Crystal Me

How to Access and Interpret Crystal Information

For Liz,

May this aid you on your journey

With love + light

Pauline

Pauline A. Wilkie
MSc, TQFE

Founder: The Phoenix College of Crystal Therapy

ISBN 978-0-9568849-0-9

First published and distributed in the UK by Crystal Phoenix Publishing

Printed and bound by Clydeside Press
www.clydesidepress.co.uk

Cover design by Pure Purple
www.purepurple.org.uk

Contents

Acknowledgements

Acknowledgements

Grateful thanks to Dr Lisa Robinson-Hall, PhD, for her unfailing commitment and clarity of vision during the final stages of completing this book.

Thanks to Dr Raymond Thomson, PhD, for his abiding enthusiasm, encouragement and support at the beginning of this journey.

For their contributions in the form of personal attunements, I should like to thank Lisa Robinson-Hall, Tracy Byron and Evelyn McFarland.

Thanks to Nicola Leslie-Gallagher, Principal of The Phoenix College of Crystal Therapy, for a continued and mutually supportive working partnership.

I should also like to thank Marion Voy, who told me several years ago to believe in myself. I have never forgotten.

Last, but not least, thanks to my husband Bill, for never complaining when I spent most of my time researching or at the computer in order to make this book happen.

Introduction

Much has been written about the therapeutic properties of crystals for health and healing, but never before has there been a clear link made between scientific research, the human energy field and the healing power of crystals.

This thought-provoking new book reveals how the results of recent research provide evidence that there *is* a scientifically clear and credible link between crystals and their use for influencing the human energy field.

The book also provides a straightforward guide to accessing the information stored in crystals, and explains how this information might be applied in everyday life to enhance and improve personal health and well-being. This knowledge is extremely valuable, at this time of heightened awareness, when more and more people are being drawn to crystals.

The opening chapter describes what happened when I accessed the information stored in a Lemurian Seed. I came across this crystal on a stall I hadn't seen before at a Body and Soul Exhibition in Glasgow several years ago. The seller told me that these crystals (there were about eight of them) had been discovered buried in the sand covering the floor of a mine in Brazil which had recently been drained. Note that they were *buried* and not actually attached to rock, as would normally be expected – it was as if they had been placed there by someone for safe-keeping. There was one crystal in particular which kept drawing my eye and, after handling all the crystals, I finally made my purchase. It is interesting to note that I actually had it in my possession for eighteen months before I felt drawn to working with it. What is even more interesting is the fact that I have never seen the stall or heard of the stallholder ever again!

The chapters which immediately follow this are intended to provide the necessary scientific background and evidence to illustrate the link between the human energy field and crystals. I appreciate that not everyone will find this interesting or easy to read; nevertheless, it is an integral and important part of the whole.

I have also included a chapter on how to 'tune in' to crystal energy, together with a selection of 'attunements', to illustrate that it is possible to access the information stored energetically in crystals and then to interpret the messages received in a meaningful way for personal use and benefit.

1: Setting the Scene

The following account describes what happened when I 'attuned' to a Lemurian Seed Crystal in order to access the information stored within it.

Further examples of attunements to a variety of different crystals can be found in Chapter 6.

Crystal: Lemurian Seed Crystal

Origin – Igneous

Colour – Clear, striated, etched

Generally held characteristics

Little is known about these amazing crystals, except that they are formed from clear quartz and are believed to have been programmed with important information from Lemurian times. It is said that they only appear when the time is right for the information they hold to be known - and then, only to the 'right' person.

Attunement message

Immediately after beginning the attunement I was transported back to ancient times – perhaps Egypt, it was

3

not clear. I was aware of being in an underground cavern lit with crude torches. I was a man, bald and tall and when I looked down at my hands I saw that they were tanned and strong but also that they were capable of great gentleness. Before me was a stone bench full of surgical instruments of the time and I knew instantly that I was a surgeon healer. To my left, someone was being carried into the room on a makeshift stretcher and the words 'plague' and 'pestilence' came to mind. The person had been blinded and I looked down at my instruments and thought that there was nothing there that would help him. However, at the very end of the stone bench my eyes alighted on a crystal – my Lemurian Seed Crystal. As soon as I saw it the words 'blindness' and 'healing' came into my mind and I knew immediately that I was being shown that I could use this crystal to help the man's blindness.

Interpretation

The crystal was showing me that in a past life I had been a surgeon healer and had known how to use such a crystal for healing a man's blindness. Lemurian Seed crystals are powerful tools and need to be used with great care, skill and integrity. This attunement indicated that I was being given permission to use it for healing because I was now at a stage where my skill and ability was sufficient to do advanced work with specialist crystals. At the time, I was working with a client who had Bell's Palsy. She had a drooping right eye which was not responding to orthodox treatment, and I knew that this would be the right crystal to use at our next meeting.

Crystal Energy and modern day use of crystals

Crystal Healing has been defined as:

'The therapeutic application of crystals and gemstones for healing the mental, physical, emotional, and spiritual bodies.'

'Crystal healing is an alternative medicine technique that employs stones and crystals as healing tools.'

'A healing energy generated by quartz and other minerals.'

'The use of the supposed power of crystals to affect the human energy field.'

(Collins English Dictionary, 2003)

While all of these definitions are in part, useful, it is this last definition, in the Collins English Dictionary, that is the most challenging.

This definition underlines the generally-held premise that there is, as yet, no substantial scientific evidence to support how crystals can be used to influence the giant energy field which surrounds and governs all matter – including the human body.

This text sets out to establish the link between crystals, the human body and the information available to it in the universal energy field - demonstrating that sufficient scientific research is now taking place to show that there *is* a credible evidence base to underpin the use of natural crystals to enhance human health and well-being.

How and why crystals work

In 1880 Jacques and Pierre Curie discovered that when certain crystalline minerals were subjected to a mechanical force, the crystals became electrically polarized. Tension and compression generated voltages of opposite polarity, in proportion to the applied force. The discovery of this unusual characteristic has resulted in many modern day inventions.

Crystals have the properties of both *piezoelectricity* and *pyroelectricity. Piezo* is Greek and means 'to squeeze', and *electrose* means 'to get a charge from. 'Piezoelectricity* is the quality whereby static electricity, and sometimes light, is produced by compression. Compression results in the release of electrons and these electrons remain on the crystal allowing it to hold the 'charge', sometimes for a long period of time. P*yroelectricity* is when a current is created by heating or cooling the crystal.

A simple analogy would be like combing your hair with a plastic comb. The act of combing causes static electricity to form. When the combing stops, if the comb is placed close to a piece of paper it will attract the paper because of the static charge held in the comb.

Similarly, this particular property is harnessed in modern medical practice. In ultrasound equipment, a *piezoelectric* transducer converts electrical energy into extremely rapid mechanical vibrations—so fast, in fact, that it makes sounds, but too high-pitched for our ears to hear. These ultrasound vibrations can be used for scanning, cleaning, and to treat serious medical conditions deep within the body – without the need for invasive surgery.

Piezoelectricity is also used, much more crudely, in spark lighters for gas stoves and barbecues. Press a lighter switch and you'll hear a clicking sound and see sparks appear. What you're doing, when you press the switch, is squeezing a *piezoelectric crystal*, generating a voltage, and making a spark fly across a small gap.

Nowadays, crystals are used in a wide range of electronic devices – most notably by Hewlett-Packard, one of the world's leading manufacturers of computers and other electronic equipment. It is only since the beginning of the 20th century that scientists have begun to harness the incredible power of crystals, particularly quartz crystal. Information is stored on tiny silicon crystal chips by using the unique properties of piezoelectric silicon dioxide, or quartz crystal.

So – if it is scientifically possible to store vast amounts of information inside modern computers using quartz crystals, and if it is possible to harness the vibrational energy of crystals for use in modern medicine, it may also be possible to utilise - with the appropriate skill and knowledge - the properties, qualities and vibrational energy of crystals for other purposes, *including the use of crystals for health and well-being.*

2: Some Contemporary Evidence

In 'The Mystery of the Crystal Skulls', Morton and Thomas (1997) refer to research conducted by Dr John Pohl, Mesoamerican specialist at the University of California and Los Angeles, who discovered on his various trips to Central America, that modern day descendants of the ancient Mayan civilisation still recognise the distinctive qualities of quartz crystal and liken it to some sort of ancient communication device. Similarly, in his introduction to the book 'Holy Ice' by Frank Dorland (1992), Dr Joseph Alioto makes an interesting comment.

He states that if less than a hundred years ago, anyone had said that there was an invisible energy force that permeates all things, and that this energy force would allow us to see and hear other people all over the world immediately, they would have been thought to be 'either a great sorcerer or a great liar.' Additionally, if it were to be suggested that these sounds and images could be received through the use of a specifically created box containing only pieces of metal and crystals, it would most likely create 'quite a stir.'

What is being referred to is something we have come to take for granted, something most homes would not nowadays be without - a television. It is difficult to believe that, until just a few generations ago, this idea was consigned to the realms of 'fantasy and science fiction.' (Dorland, 1992 p57)

Due to the unique properties of crystal, a natural piece of piezoelectric silicon dioxide (clear quartz crystal) has exactly the same capacity to store information as a silicon chip. What is important to acknowledge is that the 'information' stored on a silicon chip is not tangible, neither does it have a physical form. The only way it can be seen or heard is by retrieving it electronically.

Dorland suggests that a piece of natural piezoelectric quartz crystal is capable of interacting with the human body and human mind, but in a way that we are not normally conscious of. His theory is based on the idea that the human body and natural quartz are constantly broadcasting electromagnetic signals on an unheard wavelength, and he reminds us that we are constantly surrounded by a 'sea of electromagnetic energy waves'. For example, we cannot detect the full range of complex radiant energy produced by the sun nor can we detect the man-made electromagnetic energy waves emitted by microwaves or the television.

Dorland also points out that research has estimated that the capability for detection in the average human being is less than two per cent of the known wavelength spectrum. This would seem to suggest that we are not aware of over ninety eight per cent of what is happening around us at all times.

Furthermore, he comments that because the human body is such a complex system of both electrical and chemical networks, it is capable of transmitting and receiving signals from an innumerable diversity of sources.

Accordingly, he observes that when a human being comes into contact with a piezoelectric quartz crystal it receives the electromagnetic energy waves (signals) produced by the human body. As soon as these are received the quartz crystal begins to oscillate and amplify the signals, then resends them in a modified form back out into the atmosphere where they are picked up again by the cells of the body. Dorland's idea forms the basis of the concept that there is now a credible scientific link between the human energy field and crystals, and will be expanded on throughout this work.

His argument supports the work of the Hewlett-Packard scientists who, in the 1970's in their laboratories in Santa Clara, California, were asked to carry out tests on the Mitchell-Hedges crystal skull to determine if it genuinely was made from piezoelectric quartz crystal. Hewlett-Packard scientists were chosen to carry out these tests because of their expertise in the physical, technical and scientific properties of quartz crystal.

Their findings revealed that it was 'vertically piezo-electrically oriented' which meant that if an electrical charge was applied to the top of the skull the electric current would pass from the top of the skull straight down to the earth below. Also, because the Mitchell-Hedges skull is made from piezoelectric quartz it has both a positive and negative polarity – which means that if it is squeezed it is capable of generating electricity.

The scientists were also aware that piezoelectric silicon dioxide (quartz crystal) is highly stable in the environment. Jack Kusters, principal scientist at Hewlett-Packard at the time of the tests stated that:

'Quartz crystal is highly stable, physically, chemically and temperately, and whilst it does respond to light and electricity, this is precisely what makes it so useful in electronics.'

Quartz has the *proven ability* to hold and emit electrical energy and to oscillate at a constant and precise frequency. It is exactly these properties which make it invaluable in both modern medicine and our world of high-speed, electronically-based information and complex communications technology.

3: Subtle Energy Fields

Until a few short decades ago it was widely believed that there was no logical scientific framework to support the fact that energetic therapies rely on subtle energy field interactions. However, both academic and medical research is now able to show that the human body is able to respond, both positively and negatively, to the electromagnetic energy fields in our environment.

For many years physicists and biologists have been at odds over the effects of electricity and magnetism on living systems. This appears to be because biologists have repeatedly documented that all living systems, at all levels of organisation, have amazing sensitivity to exceedingly small signals in their environment. Living organisms, they believe, use energetic 'cues' not only to orient themselves geographically but also to detect predators and mates, to anticipate seasonal changes and also to set their biological rhythms. (Kalmijn, 1971; Adey & Bawin, 1977; Warnke, 1994).

However, physicists treat living systems like other forms of matter. They use the known laws of electricity and magnetism to calculate the currents induced in tissues by environmental fields of various sorts. These calculations are based on the degree that, amongst other things, fields of differing frequencies penetrate the body. A consistent conclusion has been that environmental fields can have no biological effect on living matter unless the energy intensity is sufficient to ionize or heat tissues. (Foster & Guy, 1986; Foster & Pickard, 1987; Wachtel, 1995).

So who is right?

Adey and Bawin (1997) reported that research undertaken by scientists from the Neurosciences Research Program has resolved this dilemma which existed between physics and biology. This research discovered that biological systems completely defy the simple logic that larger stimuli should produce large responses and some interesting conclusions were subsequently drawn.

They recounted that in experiments done under adequately considered and controlled conditions, it was discovered that a remarkable variety of biological interactions had occurred. It was revealed that the biological responses to very weak electromagnetic fields suggested the existence of an extraordinarily efficient mechanism for detecting these fields, and also for distinguishing them from much higher levels of noise.

They concluded that this underlying mechanism must inevitably involve an increasing number of components in the sensing system, and that these components were arranged in a particular way to form an effective structure capable of sensing similar levels and types of energy, even over long distances.

These findings would appear to herald the emergence of a new paradigm in biology which has led to on-going and extensive research and clinical investigation into the effects of electromagnetic fields.

Dr Valerie Hunt (2010), Emeritus Professor in the UCLA Department of Physiological Sciences and physiology researcher for 40 years, was the first to discover the relationship between changes in bio-energy fields and human behaviour and experience. Her work scientifically proves the existence of the human energy fields, and now helps us to fully understand how subtle energy healing really works.

She describes how many human diseases have previously been categorised as 'etiology unknown.' In other words, the cause of the disease could not be established, and therefore the only possible treatment was the alleviation of the symptoms. Hunt explains that physiological symptoms occur because of disturbances in the field. She advocates that if we were to correct the disturbances in the field, the symptoms would disappear and we will have been healed. However, if we only treat the symptoms, then when a stressful situation exacerbates the disturbed energy that is the source of the problem, the disease will reappear.

Dr Hunt relates that when she was at UCLA in the early '70s, one of her graduate students asked her to explain what was happening physiologically when she was involved in trance dancing, a form of dance the student had experienced during her stay in Haiti. Prior to dancing, Hunt placed sensors on the student's body which were designed to measure the muscle tissue and basic organ vibrations. What was astonishing was that the data from the electrodes showed frequencies that seemed to originate from a source other than her physical systems. The tests were repeated many times with the result that Hunt was able to conclude that she had discovered a dynamic field of energy surrounding the human body that had never before been recorded by scientific instruments.

The readings were done via bipolar contacts that took readings from the body's surface which were then fed into a small radio system and could be broadcast. The same way the nodules are used in doing an electrocardiogram (EKG), but Dr Hunt's instruments were not capable of picking up the full range and intensity of the fields she wanted to study. She explained that the Electromyogram (EMG) test instruments, for example, pick up only frequencies from 0 to 250 cycles per second (Hz); electroencephalogram (EEG) and EKG devices register only as high as 100 and 150 Hz, respectively. These tests check the electrical activity in the heart (EKG), the muscles (EMG) and the brain (EEG).

This deficiency of standard medical devices to report on the human bio-energy field led Dr Hunt to seek help from the scientists who developed telemetry devices for NASA. Postulating that human bio-energy fields oscillate at significantly higher frequencies than EKG or EEG machines were designed to measure, Dr Hunt developed a high frequency instrument which records the bio-electrical energy that emanates from the body's surface. She proved that energy radiating from the body's atoms give frequencies 1000 times faster than any other known electrical activity of the body.

As a result, a brand new research device was created for her laboratory, one which could measure frequencies from zero up to 250,000 Hz — a thousand times greater than anything ever used in medical science before that time. She has called this device the AuraMeter™. Although her AuraMeter is not yet available, this information is notable in that it provides a scientific link to the fact that this energy really does exist.

Dr Hunt's energy field data produced the first dramatic chaos patterns ever found in human biology systems. Her research is continuing to uncover the dynamic transactions that take place between humans and their environment, and begins to shed light on the effects of behaviour and emotions on health, illness and disease.

More recently, in March 2009 a documentary film emerged entitled 'The Living Matrix.' This film presents a new understanding of human biology through established scientific principles. It demonstrates the effectiveness of alternative medicine - specifically, science-based bio-energetic medicine - through the experiences of real people, even those who approached it with scepticism.

The film reveals that the body is more than a distinct machine made up of separate mechanical parts, and that energy and information fields drive physiology and biochemistry. It also illustrates how all living things are connected by energy and information fields, making wellness the result of optimal energy connections among those fields. Featured in the film are many famous names in recent scientific research, including science journalist and award-winning author of international bestsellers on quantum health, Lynne McTaggart.

The scene is set initially with a description of the scientific discoveries of Newton from which resulted the idea that the body was a machine with two engines, the heart and the brain, with the whole being controlled by the DNA. Newton believed that the universe was a very well-controlled place with separate things operating in time and space, according to fixed laws. The idea that the mind is separate from the body and that we are separate from each other appears to have become the foundation of our current western thinking. McTaggart suggests that this is the key reason why we have come to think of various processes being localised in certain parts of the body. She advocates that there now needs to be a fundamental shift from this way of thinking to the acknowledgement that the body is completely decentralised and that there is no 'central' brain. Her belief is that the brain can be likened to a transmitter and receiver of information rather than a central repository of information.

In the same film Dr Bruce Lipton, cell biologist, seems to support her belief and argues that in a conventional world of science and bio-chemistry we tend to focus on the Newtonian belief of a material world. Historically, he suggests that science has caused us to focus on the mechanical reality with the result that we have let go of the idea of energy and fields as information in biology. What he appears to be saying is that it is only matter that has become important – the rest is not. He advocates that we are now beginning to recognise that the mind is an energetic field of thought which can be measured using a technique called Magnetoencephalography (MEG). This is a non-invasive neurophysiological technique that measures the magnetic fields generated by neuronal activity of the brain.

Similarly, Peter Fraser, Chief Scientific Officer, NES, reports in the film that between 1875 and 1920 there was an enormous growth in biochemistry, and it was then thought that the human body was a *chemical* machine. If the body machine malfunctioned the answer was to put the right chemical into the machine to make it work again. He also explains that at this time there was a major intellectual debate taking place in the physics arena between the supporters of Newtonian theory and the advocates of the newly-discovered quantum physics. The result of this debate was that the old idea of a mechanical universe where everything happened for a specific reason had to be changed: however, he seems to suggest that this viewpoint has yet to be fully adopted and incorporated into our current model of biology.

Likewise, Rupert Sheldrake, biologist and Cambridge professor, also suggests in the film that the main problem with the current model of biology is that it is too mechanistic. Firstly, because it tries to explain everything in terms of molecules (the smallest things in organisms), and second, because it tries to treat the organism as a machine that works simply in terms of physics and chemistry.

Towards the end of the film, McTaggart reports that the current theory of how chemical reaction occurs in the body is through molecular collision – a bit like when two balls are thrown at the same time into a pool of water and collide instantaneously. However, she explains that it appears to be that modern physics has eliminated this paradigm and now understands that it is not matter but mind or rather the intelligent energy field which is of primary importance. Furthermore, she states that the intellectual pendulum swing seems to be moving towards the holistic rather than the individual approach to medicine, and that mind, intention and belief play a significant role in healing through their influence on the immune and endocrine system. The film highlights several case studies to demonstrate this.

This is confirmed by Dr David Hamilton PhD (2008), in his article '*The Quantum Mind*', which outlines how our mind and our thoughts affect the body. He reports that in studying that part of the brain where the brain cells can respond to free will and intention, scientists have been led to suggest that the mind is separate from the brain and interacts with it at the quantum level.

These findings have now led to the development of new scientific theories, which propose the idea that it is the mind that sends the signals to the brain, and that the brain simply acts as a receiver for the signals being sent from it.

4: How and Where we get our Energy from

Our energy system governs our total well-being. This system includes our foundation and survival instincts, our vitality and emotions, our will and personal power, our psychic and spiritual awareness. Choquette (2000) suggests that this same system is the matrix that channels our spirit into our body and allows us to express ourselves freely on the physical plane. It is widely accepted that there are many metaphysical centres of energy in the physical body. According to Simpson (1999), these are believed to be embedded in the spinal column or 'sushumna' from the coccyx to the crown and are collectively referred to as the chakra system.

This is confirmed by Rennison (2006) who highlights that an important component of our electromagnetic make-up is the central tube of energy that exists and penetrates the human energy field. This column of light and energy, which extends from the crown at the top of the head down through the body and through the perineum, is where we make fundamental connections to the Earth. Rennison indicates that it is of great importance how much energy is taken into this central tube as it directly affects how much energy is available for our body systems. She advocates that humans are made up of many layers of light and energy and that in addition to a physical body we have subtle bodies that surround and interpenetrate the physical body.

Rennison reports that scientists now acknowledge that the human body operates as a series of antennas, receiving and transmitting electromagnetic messages. If parts of the body are 'frozen', caused by unresolved emotion, then the body cannot operate or function at the optimal level. As a result, areas of the body become 'dead zones' and messages cannot be sent or received. She believes that this is why alternative medicine such as acupuncture enables healing, as blockages to the energy flow in the body are cleared.

This confirms the work of Dr John White and Dr Stanley Krippner who proposed that the universal energy field permeates all space, animate and inanimate objects, and connects all objects to each other (Brennan, 1987). It also follows the laws of harmonic induction and sympathetic resonance – the phenomenon that occurs when a tuning fork is struck, another one placed near it will begin to vibrate at the same frequency, emitting the same sound.

The significance of Quartz crystal

Dorland (1992) proposes that the *hypothalamus gland*, situated in an area of the brain the size of a lump of sugar at the base of the cerebrum, is able to pick up the energy from quartz crystals.

The hypothalamus is composed of numerous tiny clusters of nerve cells called nuclei and together with the pituitary gland, these nuclei monitor and regulate many of the body's autonomic mechanisms, endocrine activity and some somatic functions such as body temperature, food intake, water-salt balance, blood flow and sleep-wake cycle. For these reasons, and also because it acts as a link between the nervous and the endocrine systems, this gland is critical to the regulation and functioning of the chemical and electrical processes of the body. The *hypothalamus gland* is known to be influenced by the tiniest electronic impulse and Dorland believes that it is capable of receiving and filtering the oscillating energy radiated by quartz crystals. However, he points out that rarely are we aware of these energies on a conscious level.

In addition, he indicates that an exchange of energy will only occur if a crystal is 'switched on' — in much the same way as we would first have to activate an electronic instrument or machine. We know that quartz has proven piezoelectric qualities and can be 'switched on' by compressing or squeezing the crystal. The most effective way to activate a crystal, therefore, when using it for healing purposes is to hold it in the hand. Dorland believes that once activated in this way, the crystal will react to the energies it receives, and will vibrate on a frequency which is compatible, and in harmony, with the human body and brain. *It is my belief, drawn from my observation and experience of working with clients and students over the past ten years, that this is not wholly the case. I believe that crystals also have the ability to improve communication between the conscious and the sub-conscious mind.*

Recent experiments in the use of bio-feedback have proved this to be so. In such experiments, electronic equipment has been used to 'feed back' information to patients about their internal body processes with a view to helping them change their autonomic systems and therefore control conditions which were previously thought to be beyond the limits of conscious control. So, when a crystal is activated and is placed on or close to the body there *will* be an exchange of energy – but at a sub-conscious rather than at a conscious level.

Taking this a stage further, I have frequently found that crystals work at the causal rather than the symptomatic level, meaning that as they enhance communication between the conscious and sub-conscious mind an individual is made aware of what is causing the disruption to their well-being. Once awareness is created acknowledgement can follow, and once the cause is acknowledged an individual can then be encouraged to take responsibility for their own health and well-being by changing their thought-patterns or modifying actual behaviour.

I believe that it is this energetic interaction between crystals and the human energy field that can be used to help balance the neuro-endocrine system of the body and therefore optimise health and well-being.

Implications of these findings for the use of crystals as healing tools

Today, researchers theorise that the body does indeed have a field of energy known as the morphogenic field or the body field. Rupert Sheldrake (2009), professor at Cambridge University and a biologist believes that it was the analogy of magnetic fields – the discovery that if you cut up a magnet into small pieces then each piece will have its own magnetic field - that led developmental biologists to suggest the idea that this field is now crucial to understanding how organisms develop in modern-day biology. Also, he advocates that what is now needed is a field-based model of the body if we are to integrate different forms of healing into a coherent understanding. This idea is supported by Fraser and Lipton (2009) who believe that we need a field theory to explain how the complex nervous system is able to co-ordinate everything that happens in the body.

All of this would seem to suggest that our bodies are indeed connected to one giant energy field – possibly by the bio-photon, a weak emission of light which emanates from the cells of all living things. Research carried out by Professor Fritz-Albert Popp (2009) and reported in the film 'The Living Matrix' suggests that these bio-photon emissions may be controlling our body's metabolism. Lipton (2009) supports this view and argues that it is *not our genes* that are controlling our biology.

Recently, epigeneticists have discovered that it is not the information in a cell that switches it on; rather it is what is outside of the cell – the signals from the environment.

Furthermore, Rollin McCraty (2009), Director of Research at the Institute of Heartmath, explains in the same film how studies have shown that the heart responds faster than the brain to outside stimulation. From these studies it appears that the heart and brain have access to a field of information that is not bound by time and space. This is an important discovery because it supports the idea that our feelings play a significant part in our health and well-being.

We can see from this that it is becoming apparent that the control system of the body is not in the genes or chemistry, but it is in information which seems to be available in the morphogenic field. *Significantly*, if we are able to put new information into this field in the form of crystal energy, then it should be possible to positively influence and affect our health and well-being.

5: *Accessing Information in our Energy Field*

As discussed in the previous chapters, crystals have the ability to receive and transmit energy and also to store information. It is also evident from recent research that the body is capable of receiving signals and information from the morphogenic field – the vast field of energy which surrounds it. It follows, therefore, that when a crystal is placed close to the body, the energy it emits is absorbed into this morphogenic field and the properties and qualities of that crystal then become available from the field in the form of 'energetic information', which can then be utilised by the body.

SO.................can individuals with no specialist knowledge or training access the information which is stored in crystals and subsequently released into the morphogenic field, and use it for their own personal benefit?

Quite simply, 'Yes' – with a little help and some practise. In my years of teaching people how to work with crystals, one of the most amazing things they say they have experienced is learning the basic process of 'attuning' or 'tuning in' to crystal energy - and then, with a little practise, learning how to interpret the messages received during an attunement to a particular crystal.

The Attunement Process

Attunement is the process by which we seek to 'tune in' to crystal energy and access the properties and qualities of that crystal from the morphogenic field in the form of 'energetic information'. This information can then be utilised by the individual to enhance personal well-being. Sometimes the process is very quick but more often it will take time and practise to develop successful attunement techniques

Procedure for attunement to a crystal:

- Choose a quiet place where you will not be disturbed and sit comfortably in a chair – both feet on the ground with legs uncrossed. This ensures that you are 'grounded' and that there is a free flow of energy around the body

- Have a notebook and pencil to hand so you can make notes afterwards

- If you wish, play relaxing music quietly in the background

- Hold your chosen crystal in your non-dominant hand (left hand if you are right handed and vice versa)

- Focus on the breath as it enters and leaves your body. Continue until you feel relaxed and calm. Gently close your eyes.

- Visualise a small white feather on the ground just in front of your feet. As you breathe in, see it rise from the ground and hover. As you breathe out, watch it gently float down to the ground again. Repeat several times. If you find your attention wandering, gently bring it back to focus on the feather and your breathing.

- Now turn your attention to the crystal in your hand and focus intently

- In your mind, ask the crystal what its specific qualities are and how it might work with you

The crystal will communicate this information to you – usually in one of the following ways:

- words or thoughts
- images, pictures or symbols
- colours
- feelings or sensations
- smells or sounds

- Be aware of what is occurring. Try not to interpret anything at this stage.

- When you feel a sense of completion – usually when the images, colours, thoughts etc. have stopped occurring – gradually bring your awareness back to your surroundings and open your eyes

Afterwards……..write down, as accurately and as fully as possible, what happened during the attunement – no matter now bizarre or insignificant things might appear. *This is important* - because what you write will form the basis of your interpretation of the information received, and subsequently, your understanding of how you can use the information for personal benefit.

What happens if there is no exchange of information during an attunement?

Don't worry! Sometimes a crystal will not work with an individual – perhaps because the timing is not right for that person to receive the stored information. When this happens the crystal will 'shut down' and no interaction will be experienced. If this should happen, put the crystal aside and try again at a later time.

6: *Understanding Crystal Messages*

Personal attunements versus 'what I can read in a book about crystals.'

A personal attunement to a specific crystal invariably reveals information that is intended for the person doing the attunement – the information received will have significance for that individual in the context of what is happening in their life at the time of attunement.

Descriptions read in books about the therapeutic properties of crystals and how they can be used, while useful, are inclined to be general rather than specific to an individual. Perhaps a useful analogy would be like reading your horoscope in a magazine or newspaper as opposed to having your personal horoscope chart drawn up by a professional astrologer!

Attunements and interpretation of messages received

The following pages give descriptions of some of the *author's personal attunements* to a variety of crystals, done at various stages over a ten year period of working with crystals. In addition, some *attunements from former students* have been included for interest and information. These are gratefully acknowledged.

Interpretations of the information received, together with brief details of the crystal origin, colour and generally held characteristics are also included, in order to assist analysis and understanding.

Where relevant, links to life-situations at the time of the attunement have also been incorporated, again to aid understanding and to help and encourage the reader to make the links from *their* attunements to their own life situations.

Please note: All of the attunements are, necessarily, reported in the first person.

Crystal: Amethyst

Origin – Igneous

Colour – Purple

Generally held characteristics

'A stone of spirituality and contentment' (Melody, 1999). It opens and activates the crown chakra, bringing perfect peace, stability, strength and invigoration. It is useful for harmonising mind, body and spirit and connects us to higher planes by transmuting our lower energies into higher frequencies. It is an excellent stone for use during meditation.

On the physical level, amethyst gently relieves pain and tension. It can be used to cleanse and strengthen the skeletal and nervous systems, and aids hearing, the heart, cellular disorder and also the digestive and endocrine systems.

Attunement message

I visualised two white doves flying through a beautiful green forest with very tall trees. In their beaks were olive branches and they flew from the forest to some distant mountains which were surrounded by white, ethereal-looking clouds. I felt calm and completely at peace.

Interpretation

This crystal was showing me how it could be used to help us access our inner stillness and our state of innermost peace. It was also telling me that it can help us to connect with our highest levels of spirituality and consciousness, and with other realms beyond that in which we currently live.

Crystal: Apophyllite Top

Origin – Igneous

Colour – Clear

Generally held characteristics

Apophyllite reduces fear and anxiety and encourages a clam and tranquil attitude.

Physically, it aids respiratory problems, particularly asthma, and also regeneration of the skin.

Attunement message

When I asked to be shown the properties of this crystal I was told that the main property of this crystal is astral travel. I got lots of purple and felt a floating sensation but then nothing much happened. I had a headachy feeling in the third eye area and I wondered whether or not I had chosen the wrong crystal.

Interpretation

Once again, purple and the pain in the third eye area. I think I am getting a very clear message about opening my third eye chakra and further developing my psychic abilities.

As I didn't get anything else I wonder whether it was an unconscious block or simply not the right time. Perhaps I need to address this third eye issue before Astral travel is possible. The other thing is that I simply might not be ready yet.

Crystal: Aquamarine

Origin – Igneous

Colour – Blue/green

Generally held characteristics

This crystal is believed to bring order and calm in times of confusion by sharpening the intellect and filtering out unhelpful thoughts. It promotes far-sightedness and makes us dynamic and goal-oriented.

Physically, aquamarine aids the respiratory tract, allergies and has a balancing effect on the pituitary and thyroid glands.

Attunement message

When I asked the crystal to show me its properties and how it might work with me, the first thing I got was rebalancing the pituitary gland and stimulating the metabolism. I felt a tingling in my throat. Then I was in an operating theatre. I saw someone in a green gown and I was not sure who was on the table. I got a sense of the crystal preventing the operation or being used to ease the pain and discomfort. Next, I saw a bright spot of light in the distance surrounded by purple and magenta. I had a soothing, gentle, calm, warm feeling inside. I saw the third eye again and was aware of the need for development of psychic awareness. This was followed by purple, which was surrounded by bright white light. When I asked if there was anything else I got, 'cleanses or balances emotions.' Once the attunement was finished I was coughing for a bit.

Interpretation

The tingling in my throat could be linked to my thyroid gland, which is often underactive. This would fit with the properties of the crystal as the pituitary gland needs to be balanced in order for all the other hormones in the body to function properly. At the time I did this attunement I felt that the significance of the operating theatre could be one of three things.

First, I felt it could be some kind of a message about my Mum's illness and possibly using the crystal to prevent the need for a biopsy on the liver, or indeed further surgery. The second was that the scene was fairly similar to one I had experienced over 12 months ago in what I can only describe as an out of body experience. The third was evaluating the idea of an operation, and the fact that it could symbolise something being removed in order for me to grow or develop. Somebody else has to be involved in this scenario as you can't operate on yourself!

In a funny way I think that all three explanations are plausible. The first one is interesting as this was the crystal that Mum and I were both drawn to for her to place on the area where she was suffering a lot of pain, what I now realise was the poor liver function. She held this crystal on her side a couple of times to help ease the pain and discomfort. This is directly linked to the properties in the attunement. The second scenario, in other words, the out of body experience was what stimulated the start of my journey into holistic therapies and encouraged me to consider further spiritual development. I feel that this is possibly a reminder that I trusted last time and have come this far, therefore I need to trust again and I will grow and develop even more. Thirdly, something being removed and someone else involved.

Well, now that Mum has passed over, I wonder if this could be what is meant here. I started my crystal therapy course in order to give Mum comfort and to try to help her. I saw what a tremendous impact the crystals and the healing, including distance healing, had on her. She did not shed a tear, appeared to be fearless and was so very, very brave. I have never had any doubts about my crystal therapy course, but I did when I first trained in angel therapy, reiki and hands on healing. Mum, however, always reassured me saying how much better she felt after she had any of these therapies from me. I feel that this is reassurance to continue on this path and perhaps I could only accept their benefits by experiencing the impact they had on my Mum. By removing her from my life I am even more adamant to progress these therapies, thereby continuing to grow and develop spiritually.

After the operating theatre scene I saw the bright purple and white light. Linking to my higher self and encouraging me to open both my third eye and crown chakras in order to facilitate psychic development.

Crystal: Aventurine

Origin – Igneous

Colour – Green

Generally held characteristics

Aventurine is a member of the quartz family and owes its green, sparkling appearance to the deposits of mica or hematite in its formation. Green aventurine activates, clears and protects the heart chakra, balances yin/yang energies and is good for healing disorders of the lungs, heart and adrenal glands. It also has an anti-inflammatory effect and helps with skin diseases and eruptions, as well as alleviating pain.

Attunement message

I visualised a silvery lake, sometimes shimmering green, bordered by tall grasses and reeds. Flocks of geese were flying low over the lake but they made no sound at all. Everything was still and silent, as if viewed through glass.

Interpretation

The colours silver and green symbolise links to the crown and heart chakras, suggesting the heart and emotions can draw on the energies of the crown chakra to help us to attune to our own higher knowing.

The low-flying geese symbolise strength, calm and balance – suggesting this stone can help me to rise above my emotions (symbolised by water) and so access my higher knowing and intellect. Geese, we know, migrate, and always find their way.

The silence seems to suggest that the answers to our questions can often come through being still and silent, by remaining detached from external influences, and through listening to our inner wisdom.

Crystal: Aventurine

Origin – Igneous

Colour – Yellow

Generally held characteristics

In addition to the characteristics already described for green aventurine, yellow aventurine has an affinity with solar plexus chakra. It dissolves stress and tension and is emotionally calming and stabilising.

Attunement message

As is normal for me the attunement started with my being given the properties of the crystal. I was told the properties are – calm, peace, and serenity. I saw an image of an eye drawing me towards it. There were lots of magenta/purple colours. Then I saw a gorgeous white unicorn.

After that there were swirls of grey (negativity) rising and drifting away from my body. There was a bright spot of magenta amidst the grey and I got a sense of this being brightness in the centre as negativity clears away. This was followed by the colours magenta and indigo.

When I asked if is there was anything else, I heard the words, 'teach, tolerance and trust.' I had gurgling in my tummy during and after the attunement and had a little tingling on the right hand side of my neck. Once the gurgling and tingling had finished I felt a lovely sense of calm, and was relaxed, and de-stressed. There was an image of a white bird flying upwards and the crystal heated up very strongly.

Interpretation

This stone obviously has a very calming effect with its properties being calming, peacefulness and serenity. The unicorn symbolises something which is magical, mythical, and mystical. Perhaps it is one of my spirit guides?

The swirls of grey rising off my body represent emotional clearing, and emotional freedom. I have been feeling bogged down emotionally, making it difficult for me to get in touch with my higher self. The bright amidst the grey illustrates light at the end of the tunnel as the negativity clears away. The magenta and indigo symbolise the opening of my third eye and the stimulation of my intuition/psychic ability once the negativity has been released.

The tolerance and trust indicates that I could use this stone to teach me tolerance and help me learn to trust again. The gurgling and tingling represent areas where healing energy has gone to replace the negative energy, which has lifted off.

I feel that the white bird flying upwards at the end symbolises purity, freedom, the ability to flourish and fly, soaring upwards. The crystal heating up very strongly is probably a sign that it was working with me to rebalance my solar plexus chakra and heal any pain and negativity.

Crystal: Calcite

Origin – Sedimentary

Colour – Brown

Generally held characteristics

Calcite releases electrical impulses when placed under pressure, and is an energy amplifier when an appropriate colour is placed on the chakra. This has the effect of clearing, activating and re-energising a blocked or sluggish chakra. It is generally held that calcite is a world teacher for all humanity, facilitating macrocosmic awareness by taking us 'out of the fast lane', so that we have the time to notice and acknowledge our rightful place in the system and order of things. Physically, calcite stimulates the metabolism, fortifies the immune system and encourages healing of tissue and bone.

Attunement message

I visualised a massive black hole going deep into the Earth. Orange and red flames appeared out of the hole, dying down eventually to leave bare earth. New trees sprang out of the bare soil and I noticed birds were singing in the branches.

Interpretation

This crystal was showing me that it can help us to connect to and feel part of the collective here on Earth. Also, it was showing me how it can be used to speed up processes, encouraging growth and development on all levels.

Crystal: Calcite

Origin – Sedimentary

Colour – Pale yellow

Generally held characteristics

As previously described, calcite slows us down and takes us 'out of the fast lane.' Yellow calcite is said to intensify the energy of the solar plexus chakra, helping to 'kick start' it after removing blockages. It is an excellent stone for assisting with problems associated with the dysfunction of the pancreas, kidneys, stomach and spleen.

Attunement message

When attuning to this crystal I also used colour breathing to enhance the effects of the yellow calcite. I breathed deeply, visualising yellow light flooding into my solar plexus and immediately saw this chakra as a dandelion clock. As I breathed out, one by one the seeds of the clock were released and floated away. I was aware that the tension in this area of my body was also being released. As I continued to breathe in the yellow ray I saw the last of the dandelion seeds float away and with them the last of my tension, leaving me with a feeling of calm, peace and lightness.

Interpretation

This crystal was showing me how it can be used to dissolve blockages and negativity at the solar plexus chakra, gently helping us to let go and release tension. It will help us to slow down – taking us out of the fast lane, so that we have time to recover our balance and equilibrium on an energetic level.

Crystal: Calcite

Origin – Sedimentary

Colour – Honey

Generally held characteristics

In addition to the properties already described for calcite, honey calcite has a warming, comforting energy. It facilitates macrocosmic awareness and encourages appreciation of the natural world.

Attunement message

The crystal felt warm in my hand, melting into my palm and the heat spreading along my arm. I visualised myself driving along the road, enjoying the scenery. A bus came along behind me. The words 'slow down, why the hurry?' came into my head.

Interpretation

This crystal was soothing and warming, reminding me that I have a choice – the fast lane or the slow lane. Which way do I want to live my life? I never really thought about using this crystal for the base chakra, but now realise that it would be suitable for grounding, protection, pace and foundation for life – fast or slow? It is a crystal which will provide me with thinking space to allow things to surface naturally and with ease.

Crystal: Carnelian

Origin – Igneous

Colour – Dark orange

Generally held characteristics

Carnelian is a form of chalcedony and as such exhibits the nurturing characteristics of brotherhood, goodwill and benevolence. In addition, carnelian is believed to increase physical energy, personal power, creativity and passion. When used on the sacral chakra, it can assist in disorders of the male and female reproductive organs and will also stimulate the absorption of minerals in the small intestine.

Attunement message

I visualised myself as I was when seven or eight years old, on a swing in the park. It was a beautiful summer's day – blue sky, white clouds scudding high. The park was crowded with children, all laughing and screaming in delight and having a good time. As I swung higher and higher, I screamed too – yet felt no fear, and the breeze ruffled my hair as it 'whooshed' past my ears. I felt happy, elated, excited and light-hearted.

Interpretation

This crystal was showing me that it can work with us to uplift our emotions and release the inner child, bringing joy and enjoyment into our lives. It is also a protective stone (I had felt no fear) and can bring us strength, increase our energy and stimulate our enthusiasm for life.

Crystal: Celestite

Origin – Sedimentary

Colour – Pale blue

Generally held characteristics

Celestite is excellent for facilitating mental activities – particularly for getting to grips with complex ideas and analysis. It brings calmness and harmony, lifting the spirits and improving the 'feel good' factor.

It is also a stone which facilitates contact with the angelic realms and assists astral travel.

Physically, it treats disorders of the eyes and ears, eliminates toxins and brings cellular order.

Attunement message

It took a long time to 'tune in' to this cluster of beautiful, pale blue crystals and the visualisation, when it came, was brief. I saw a mountain peak with two cherub-like angels on either side, blowing long trumpets, a bit like the kind we see on Christmas cards!

Interpretation

A very clear message, that this crystal can help us to access the angelic or spiritual realms.

Crystal: Charoite

Origin – Metamorphic

Colour – Purple

Generally held characteristics

Charoite has the ability to stimulate our mental faculties, bringing clarity and mental acuity when faced with important decision-making. It acts as a relaxant, soothing the nerves while at the same time helping to put things into perspective so that they can be dealt with vigorously and with determination.

Physically, charoite has a pain-relieving effect and also alleviates cramps.

Attunement message

Initially I saw a large fin moving in dark water, then the back of what looked like a dinosaur. My eyes followed the body up the long neck which rose up into the air to become a pterodactyl, flying in a different direction. My vision became watery, I was looking through and into water which became rain filling up the surrounding area. The rain stopped and only a puddle remained, which quickly dried up and was gone.

Interpretation

Charoite is a metamorphic crystal and has the ability to show us that nothing is constant. I was taken back two hundred million years to the Jurassic period where I was shown a slow moving, large dinosaur, which made me think of a diplodocus, a slow moving herbivore. I was that dinosaur plodding along slowly with no great purpose, whereas now I am the pterodactyl flying high, changing direction and moving on. Moving water symbolises life and vitality, the rain being moving water. It also releases negative ions which give a positive atmosphere. Rain and moving water also attract chi energy, giving energy for life. The rain stopped and the puddle dried up to give me a clear path without hurdles, showing the way forward.

Crystal: Citrine

Origin – Igneous

Colour – Yellow

Generally held characteristics

A stone of the solar plexus chakra, citrine stimulates and energises the physical body, especially the thymus. It is excellent for improving circulation, treating tumours, degenerative disorders, and balancing yin/yang energies. It brings comfort and optimism and promotes inner radiance. It does not hold or accumulate negative energy and therefore never needs cleansing. Also, it is useful for attracting and maintaining wealth, promoting group or family cohesiveness and positively influencing education and business. It is known as the 'stone of abundance' or 'the merchant's stone' – however, it tends to attract what we need which is not always the same as what we want.

Attunement message

I visualised a lion – regal, strong and handsome, walking slowly and serenely then lying and stretching in the hot sun. I noticed that the focus of the visualisation was on the lion's face, clearly showing great inner strength, self-contentment and a sense of peace and wholeness.

Interpretation

The crystal was showing me that it could help me to access my inner strength by opening and energising the solar plexus chakra. Having done this, it can then help to energise and enhance on all levels – physically, emotionally and mentally – so that I can fully acknowledge my personal power and potential by being all I can be.

Crystal: Emerald

Origin – Igneous

Colour – Green

Generally held characteristics

Emerald belongs to the beryl family and as such assists in speeding up our rate of vibration. Crystals belonging to this family strengthen our etheric structure and help us to align to the Light and our purpose in this lifetime.

Emerald encourages spiritual growth, emotional regeneration and mental clarity and wakefulness.

On the physical level, it improves the ability to see, heals inflammations of the sinuses and upper respiratory tract, fortifies the heart and is generally detoxifying.

Attunement message

I visualised myself spreading pale green ointment over someone's chest. Although the chest was not mine, I could feel the effects of the ointment which were soothing, cooling (like menthol) and the words 'healing' and 'restorative' came to mind.

Interpretation

This crystal was showing me that it can be used to detoxify and also to heal and strengthen the heart and respiratory system.

Crystal: Faden Quartz

Origin – Igneous

Colour – Colourless with a white, thread-like inclusion

Generally held characteristics

The name 'Faden' is derived from the German translation of 'thread.' It is a crystal of connection, linking one person to another, regardless of time or place. It enhances clairvoyance, clairaudience and clairsentience.

It aids mental and emotional stability and is said to be useful in cases of epilepsy, schizophrenia and drug-related conditions.

Attunement message

Initially, I saw a young woman, the Deva of this crystal, wearing a cloak with a hood. When she removed her cloak and hood I saw that she was wearing a long, floating dress and had long, blonde curls. When I asked if she had anything to show me, she pushed aside an enormous boulder. She then flew up into the clouds and I saw light emerge from each side of her as wings emerged from her back, like an angel. I visualised my third eye looking at me, then I saw a black triangle emerge from under the clouds. I asked her who or what I needed to connect to so that I could progress on my spiritual path. I saw the head of Darth Vader.

Interpretation

The crystal was making me aware that we cannot take anything at face value, but it is important to have faith. Things we cannot see may intimidate us or make us curious, therefore she revealed her beauty and strength, by physically removing her cloak and by moving the huge boulder.

Although faden quartz may not outwardly be the most beautiful crystal, inside it is stunning and powerful. I feel the Deva was also making me aware that sometimes I am kept back by hurdles, as symbolised by the boulder. However, I am in control and can move these hurdles aside to allow me to continue on my path. With the assistance of faden quartz I can ascend and move forward on my path of personal development. The appearance of the third eye was a message to have faith and trust my intuition, as quite often I do not have faith in myself or trust my inner thoughts.

The upwards pointing triangle is indicative of yang energy, the masculine, strong, more aggressive element, whereas black is the colour associated with yin energy. However, black is also considered the colour of 'letting go.' On asking her who or what I needed to connect to she showed me the head of Darth Vader. In the Star Wars films Anakin Skywalker became consumed by the dark side to become Darth Vader. However, before he died the good in him came through while in the company of his son, Luke Skywalker, a Jedi of the forces of good. I feel my Deva was showing me that there is good in bad, that we all have a shadow side and that it is alright to be strong and in control, but not to let power consume us.

Crystal: Fluorite

Origin – Igneous

Colour – Purple

Generally held characteristics

Fluorite helps dissolve rigid patterns of thought and behaviour, increasing the ability to think more freely and with discernment. Mentally, it improves concentration and stimulates quick thinking and the processing of information.

On the physical level, fluorite strengthens teeth and bones, improves joint mobility and benefits skin regeneration.

Attunement message

Almost immediately I felt a pulsing sensation throughout my body and my lower jaw and teeth felt clenched. I visualised the tree of knowledge and felt as if I was 'plugged in' to a source of power. My whole body felt vibrant and energized. This was a very quick and powerful attunement.

Interpretation

The pulsing feeling was reassuring and emotionally stabilising. I felt that the 'tree' was pointing me towards books and to study, showing me that I need to use all of my senses to gain further knowledge.

This will be a good crystal to use to help me study and to keep me mentally stimulated and alert.

Crystal: *Fluorite Octahedron*

Origin – Igneous

Colour – Purple

Generally held characteristics

Fluorite enhances realisation of our highest potential. It initiates and transforms by pushing us through our limitations and it takes us unto new awakenings. It assists the flow of energy into the third and fourth dimensions.

The octahedron shape enhances fluorite's natural ability to help us flow with the Divine Plan and brings in the energy of the two pyramids – initiation and transformation.

It is highly protective and cleansing, is able to eliminate negativity on all levels and also to reduce trauma.

Attunement message

I heard and felt a cold wind blowing across a frozen wasteland and visualised myself standing in this wasteland wearing a hooded, furry jacket. My face felt frozen and the light was very dim. It was as if I was standing inside the crystal itself.

Two husky dogs cuddled up to me, one on either side, to keep me warm. They started to lick my face and I felt loved and protected. Eventually, the sun began to rise over the horizon, bringing warmth and pure white/purple light. The dogs and I turned and walked together towards the sunrise.

Interpretation

This crystal was showing me the two extremes needed to bring personal balance. On the one hand – self-sufficient, distant, excluding of others as symbolised by the frozen wasteland. On the other – the dogs were there to remind me that there will be times when I need the help of others to bring me to wholeness.

The crystal was teaching me that it takes strength not only to be self-sufficient and to stand alone, but also to allow ourselves to be vulnerable and to let others see our vulnerability. A valuable realisation.

Crystal: Garnet (pyrope)

Origin – Metamorphic

Colour – Deep red

Generally held characteristics

Garnet is particularly good at bringing more light into the base and other lower chakras, encouraging clearer connections between the lower and higher selves and also between the physical self and the Divine Blueprint. These crystals are the classic stones of crisis, helping us to cope with and surmount everyday problems in extreme situations. Garnet fortifies the desire for self-realisation and encourages the vision to see more than our own narrow horizon. It brings confidence, courage, hope, trust and *joie de vivre*.

Attunement message

The crystal felt cold and heavy in my hand. I visualised a bonfire with leaping orange, red and yellow flames. All around was darkness and quiet – there was not even any sound from the leaping flames. I saw a dark, faceless figure being consumed by the flame, but the figure made no sound. Almost immediately, the figure changed to a young woman with long, golden hair. She was dressed in white, with a pale blue gem-encrusted girdle at her waist, a pale blue cloak and she wore a coronet.

Her hair and the colours of her clothes reminded me of myself when I was about eight years old – except that her costume was of the mediaeval period. The flames of the fire were not touching her, and she smiled serenely and looked calm and untroubled. I asked to meet the crystal Deva and visualised a darkly-clad figure with a saint-like face. Around her head was a halo, perhaps her aura, of golden light. I asked for clarification of my visualisation and she said, 'inner peace will be yours.'

Interpretation

This crystal was showing me how it could help me access past life knowledge, and use this knowledge to help me move from one phase of my current life to the next. It is a stone of transition.

The crystal took me to two of my past lives – the first when I was being burned at the stake, possibly as a witch. The second, I was a young woman, possibly of royal connection, as symbolised by the crown.

The important thing was that the transition from one life to another was smooth, fearless and without pain, and this was reinforced by the colours white and pale blue.

Crystal: Garnet (spessartine)

Origin – Metamorphic

Colour – Red/brown

Generally held characteristics

Spessartine garnet is believed to be one of the finest crystals to help individuals speak openly and frankly about anything that is considered taboo. It strengthens willpower and determination, and on a physical level, aids the heart and immune system.

Attunement message

I felt very strong vibrational energies in the chest area and had a panicky sensation. I was immediately transported back to a scene from my childhood (when I was six or seven) and it was very vivid and very clear. It was a hot day and I was at my friend's house (a neighbours) playing in their back garden. My paddling pool was there and I was wearing a cerise pink bikini. My friend's dad called me into the living room and lifted me onto his knee. He then started to abuse me, so I ran away into the back garden. I then heard, 'Release let go. It is ok to enjoy sex. It isn't dirty or evil. When this happens there will be renewed confidence. Relax.' After that I saw an orange dot, followed by purple and red. I then heard, 'release the passion, don't hold anger.'

I felt a nice, warm, light energy. It was very feminine and the attunement ended with the word 'transformational'.

Interpretation

I had not thought about that incident for a long time but if I am honest it is something I have carried around with me for many years. Always trying to convince myself that I hadn't been a victim of assault/abuse, as I had managed to escape before he had the chance to rape me. I also felt guilty for never reporting it to the police as I worried, once I grew up and realised the severity of what had happened, that this man was free to do this, and perhaps something worse to other girls. I guess this attunement was a wake-up call to let me know that I was carrying this around as baggage subconsciously and that I needed to release and let go of it. I feel that I have actually done this and felt better simply from the attunement itself, but also after a conversation I had with a colleague (who had also been abused), who made me realise that I actually was a victim. In a strange way that helped me to accept what had happened and to deal with it.

The orange colour is linked to the sacral chakra, the centre of sexuality/passion, pleasure, joy, well-being and physical movement. This was perhaps a clearing of the chakra and a rebalancing. The red is linked to the base chakra, representing safety, security, survival, stability, physical energy, and logic. All of these things would be rebalanced as a result of the clearing/healing taking place at the sacral chakra and also emotionally. I think this is reflective of me letting go of the insecurities linked to the incident, therefore bringing about balance and equilibrium in my attitude to/opinion of sex.

All I can say about this is that the crystal was, as it said, 'transformational', and in dealing with what had happened in the past, through the use of this crystal, I feel much better indeed, completely transformed.

Crystal: Himalayan Quartz Diamond

Origin – Igneous

Colour – Clear, colourless, bright

Generally held characteristics

A variety of quartz found in the Himalayan region, this stone has extreme, diamond - like brilliance and high vibrational energy. This is a crystal to bring clarity and Light, and can be used to promote spiritual growth and development. It cleanses and purifies on all levels, dissolving negativity and enhancing energy.

Attunement message

Properties – spiritual consciousness, clarity, personal self-development. Then I heard the statement 'it will allow you to fly.'

The colour magenta with the diamond in a three - dimensional view, spinning and vibrating. The energy was very powerful and very high indeed. I felt a sensation of flying or floating upwards. Then I was flying on the back of a white unicorn. The unicorn became a duck and then a dove, which flew away. This was followed by the colour magenta again and an eye drawing me inwards. It was a very magical, mystical, experience. Next, I saw strong pure white light in the distance which then changed to magenta (a brilliant hue) with smog rising and clearing. When I asked is there anything else? I heard, 'allow to fly!!' and 'Divine guidance.' Afterwards, I felt as if I was floating and needed to be grounded.

Interpretation

This attunement is representative of the typical properties of Himalayan Quartz Diamond, which brings clarity and light, cleanses/energises on all levels and encourages spiritual growth. I believe the crystal was showing me its ability to help me 'to reach new heights.' It would therefore be excellent to use to assist with personal growth and spiritual development. The unicorn, for me, represents something very magical and mystical. I have been told before that I have a unicorn working with me as a guide and this attunement was perhaps re-confirming that for me.

In addition the transformation of the duck to a dove symbolises ugly to beautiful; sad to happy; heavy to light; indicating the ability to use this crystal to re-energize and brighten situations and moods. It also shows that by allowing spiritual development to take place things will only get better! This was reinforced by the smog rising and clearing, which symbolises releasing/lifting of blockages.

I needed grounding after this attunement because of the fast, high vibrational energies.

Crystal: Herkimer Diamond

Origin – Igneous

Colour – Colourless, clear

Generally held characteristics

A unique form of quartz, this pseudo-diamond was discovered in Herkimer, NY, USA. It is an exceptionally high vibration stone with the ability to release, clear and promote energy on all levels. It is believed to stimulate clairvoyance, clairaudience and telepathy, and is sometimes referred to as 'the attunement stone.' This is because it can be used to attune oneself with another person or environment.

Attunement message

This was a slightly different attunement as we were working in pairs. One person placed the tip of their index finger on one point of the Herkimer diamond, and the other person did the same but touched the opposite point of the diamond.

The crystal started moving back and forward as if pushing energy between us. Visualisation of the crystal/diamond spinning in 3D. I had an overwhelming feeling of wanting to cry, followed by a swallowing sensation and the need to cough. Immediately after this there was a strong heat in my right hand. A short time later there was a slight lifting of heaviness from my heart.

I then was able to sense a golden light in the aura. This was followed by an energy surge in my right arm and a subsequent feeling of both of our auras merging and radiating golden light. A feeling of unconditional love for humanity and healing the planet, then the Sacred Geometry symbol – The Vitruvian Man.

Interpretation

The crystal moving back and forward was the energy of both individuals connecting/linking through the Herkimer diamond. The person I was working with is quite closed. I believe that the Herkimer diamond enabled me to connect with this individual and I have subsequently interpreted part of this attunement as my colleague's thoughts, feelings and emotions.

My perception is that she is holding a lot of deep-rooted anger, hurt, pain and resentment, which she is unable to release or let go of and therefore attempts to 'cover up' by trying to appear as though everything is wonderful and perfect. This often results in her 'putting on a front' and other forms of 'false' behaviour so she can maintain control. I believe that my overwhelming feeling of wanting to cry was my experiencing her extreme pain, heartache and internal sadness. I was swallowing lots, confirming the fact that she suppresses her emotions, and then I felt as if I needed to cough highlighting her need to release these emotions. I immediately felt a strong heat in my right hand, which is my dominant hand and the one I use when 'channelling' energy for healing. Perhaps this was an indication that I had connected to the healing channel and was sending healing out to my colleague. After a while, the feeling of heaviness and sadness started to lift slightly and I hope this was an indication that the healing energy was starting to work.

On the other hand, all of this may have been to do with my own thoughts feelings and emotions linked to my own sadness and grief after losing my Mum. If this was the case, then the swallowing was an indication of my suppressed emotions at the time and my own need to release and grieve properly. The coughing would therefore confirm this and indicate a release or shift, which resulted in the subsequent lifting of heaviness from my heart.

However, I believe that both of the above scenarios are true and that 'synchronicity' meant we were supposed to be working together as we were sharing similar thoughts, feelings and emotions at the time, although these were caused, I know, by completely different circumstances! Interestingly, my colleague refused to admit any of the attunement being linked to her and said that it was all about me and that she had connected straight to my psyche during the attunement and was analysing me! 'Why would any of it be about her when everything in her life was absolutely fine?' This reaction and refusal to admit any issues confirms her behaviour described above.

The remainder of the attunement highlights my view of it being a joint experience for both of us, as the energy surge and merging of our auras resulted in golden light being radiated out into the world. The Vitruvian Man symbolised divine proportion and unity. This is an indication of how two people combining their positive energy can restore harmony and balance, and emphasises the need for us to work together with others who are like-minded to send unconditional love out into the universe.

70

Crystal: Jasper

Origin – Igneous

Colour – Red

Generally held characteristics

Jasper belongs to the chalcedony family and as such possesses the ability to bring calm, peace and inner wisdom. Chalcedonies encourage brotherhood and goodwill and open us up to our infinite and boundless energy by freeing us from the limitations of our lower self. Red jasper has the ability to stimulate the circulation and flow of energy, restoring courage, determination and action. In ancient times it was considered to be 'the stone of warriors.'

Attunement message

I experienced an intense heaviness in my whole body, as if I was being dragged down into the ground. I noticed that my breathing had slowed right down and I felt unseen hands pressing on my shoulders. I visualised something wrapped in what looked like rags – it was a baby wrapped in swaddling clothes and there were yellow flames eating up the rags. The baby became a sunflower and the flames were its yellow petals. The sunflower had a face and it smiled and looked happy.

Interpretation

This crystal was showing me how it could help to ground me, to take me out of the fast lane and slow me down. The symbolism of the baby and the sunflower was to show me how it could help me to shed outworn ideas, thoughts and emotions – all the limitations of my lower-self personality which might be inhibiting my personal growth. It also showed me that by doing this I would be ready to be reborn, and so embrace the new opportunities and new possibilities for my development.

Crystal: Jasper (turitella)

Origin – Sedimentary

Colour – Green/brown with fossil markings

Generally held characteristics

Turitella jasper is formed from find-grained quartz which contains fossilised snail shells. It protects against environmental pollution and enhances detoxification and elimination.

Attunement message

The attunement started quickly with my being shown electromagnetic smog, and pointed to the electricity cables outside my house. I saw black clumps or clouds floating along through the colour purple. I had a headachy feeling, a pulsating sensation in my head and my shoulders felt very tense. I saw an image of myself sitting at my computer at work and had a gurgling in my tummy. Then I saw a purple/magenta colour and what resembled a circle of people or a ring of protection.

Interpretation

I feel that this attunement was showing me the need to protect myself against electromagnetic smog from both the electricity cables outside my house and my computer at work. This is an excellent crystal for protecting against electromagnetic smog and would therefore be extremely useful for this. Perhaps placing a turitella jasper on my computer at work would prove beneficial too.

The gurgling in my tummy was energy rebalancing in the solar plexus chakra. The circle of people/ring of protection is perhaps reminding me to protect myself from negativity and may indicate that a turitella jasper could be used to help me do this effectively. In fact, it would probably be very useful in protection from any kind of environmental pollution.

Crystal: Kyanite

Origin – Metamorphic

Colour – Light blue

Generally held characteristics

According to Melody, (1995), kyanite never needs cleansing because it does not accumulate negative energy. It has the ability to align all chakras and all subtle bodies, bringing immediate balance to the entire system. It dispels anger and frustration, stimulates communication and psychic awareness, and facilitates mental clarity.

Attunement message

I visualised blue sky with shafts of silver light radiating from a bright white cloud and felt tingling in my left hand, like tiny spears prodding me into awareness. I felt a strong sense of being able to articulate the plethora of things which had been eating away at me on all levels for some time now.

Interpretation

This crystal was showing me that it can assist in cutting through the fog when we find it difficult to understand what is happening to us. Then, having brought clarity and understanding, it can help us to put into words our interpretation of this new level of understanding, by stimulating our desire and ability to communicate.

Crystal: Lapis Lazuli

Origin – Metamorphic

Colour – Deep Blue with pyrite inclusions

Generally held characteristics

With its affinity to both the throat and the third eye chakras, Lapis Lazuli is often considered to be *the* stone of self-awareness, truth and wisdom. Physically, it helps with problems of the throat and neck and also can be used to lower blood pressure.

Attunement message

When I asked to be shown the properties of this crystal I was told that they are: meditation, communication, good for the throat chakra, and that the crystal has a high vibrational frequency. The attunement started with a variety of colours – purple, magenta, indigo, and violet.

There was a very bright light in the distance. I tried to go towards the light but it disappeared or was blocked. I got a sense of, 'relax and don't try so hard.' Then I saw my third eye and the light again. When I asked if there was anything else, I received, 'psychic awareness, meditation, ascension to Spirit guide/s.' I felt myself surrounded by a protective blanket.

Interpretation

All of the colours in this attunement are linked to the third eye and crown chakras. This is indicative of spiritual development, intuition, insight, inner wisdom, imagination, psychic ability, and higher consciousness.

I felt that this attunement was encouraging me to open these chakras and be more receptive to spiritual development. I need to relax and have confidence, which will release the block and enable me to move forwards towards the light and my Divine purpose.

I also need not be afraid as I now know that I am surrounded by a protective blanket, and that I can use this crystal as a talisman for protection.

Crystal: Malachite

Origin – Sedimentary

Colour – Dark green, banded

Generally held characteristics

A stone of transformation, malachite has a powerful energy and should therefore be used with care. It has the ability to bring to the surface deep seated issues and emotions with great rapidity, but does not support the user in dealing with these.

On the physical level, it stimulates the liver to release toxins thereby reducing acidity in the tissues. It also relieves cramp and aids arthritis.

Attunement message

This crystal is linked to deep rooted thoughts and emotions. I understood that for me these were manifesting in physical problems with my ovaries.

It was dark for quite a while. Then two dots of light came in the distance. One went out, and it was a while before any other colours came through. I started thinking about my Dad and his behaviour towards me when I was a child. He was very strict. I was asked to consider a possible link between this and my weight problem? Also, about how I felt stupid, particularly at maths.

Then I saw purple and was asked to think about my current relationship – am I repeating old patterns of behaviour? He is not treating me properly at the moment. Should I consider similarities between him and my ex-husband?

I had a gurgling in my tummy, in the lower abdomen. Then I saw purple again, with the third eye. When I asked if there was anything else I got, 'not ready.' I felt headachy and had a pain in the back of my neck.

Interpretation

The first thing I thought when I read this attunement was, wow, if I had analysed this immediately after experiencing it, as I should have done, I would not have appreciated the extent of what this crystal was trying to show me. Again, it is all down to timing and perhaps I am more ready to listen now. It doesn't make it any easier to write up though! I think this crystal was trying to show me how I have unknowingly held on to things from my childhood, which I need to deal with, and let go of, in order to grow and develop. When I was interpreting the link between malachite and my ovaries, I thought it was very strange as malachite is linked to the heart chakra but, as I am well aware, the root cause of my sacral chakra problems is very strongly linked to deep seated emotions.

The black and then the two white lights, one going out, is very poignant for me now. I believe the two lights represent my parents, and the one going out is linked to my Mum's recent death. My Dad was fairly strict with me as a child, Mum was the 'soft' one. Dad was determined that I would not be spoilt (being an only child and the first grandchild). He wanted me to appreciate everything in life and to know right from wrong, so I suppose his approach to my upbringing could be viewed as fairly autocratic. He wanted the best for me but was not always good at expressing his emotions. Consequently, I often felt like I did not meet his expectations. However, since my Mum died, my relationship between myself and my Dad has changed quite dramatically. We speak on the 'phone every day, the way Mum and I did, and Dad is no longer afraid of showing or discussing his emotions.

This crystal made me realise that the men I have been attracted to so far in my life, were domineering and controlled me to some degree. It made me think about how these relationships reflected the father - daughter relationship and drew my attention to the fact that this should not be the case in partnerships, which are about equality and give and take. I have always been the giver, in the past and perhaps not received as much back as I should have. I got a real sense of 'deserving better' and not 'settling for second best', which at the time of this attunement I could easily have done.

Since this attunement I have started a new relationship, which is completely different to any I have been in before. I feel this crystal has helped me to break old patterns of behaviour and would therefore recommend it to anyone looking to break-free from old habits or learned patterns of behaviour which no longer serve them.

Crystal: Moonstone

Origin – Igneous

Colour – White/orange

Generally held characteristics

Moonstone belongs to the Feldspar family. Feldspars help us to reach our highest levels of energy and potential and to integrate these into our lower personality. They are transformative and help us become multi-dimensional beings. They encourage us to let go of old patterns of thought and behaviour and bring us the strength and courage to move forward, often into untried and untested territory. Their attributes can be readily summed up by the phrase:

'Do not follow where the path may lead; go instead where there is no path and leave a trail.'

Attunement message

I visualised a sidewalk with children skateboarding and a park with lots of people, all enjoying themselves. The scene changed and I was inside a snowstorm globe (the ornamental type that can be shaken to see it 'snow'). I was alone, except for a snowman. At first I found it fun to run about and throw snowballs, but then I realised that I was a prisoner and couldn't get out of the globe.

Interpretation

The crystal was showing me that it can help me to work on opening myself up to humanity and all that humanity has to offer. It was telling me that 'no man is an island' and that we all need to share love and to be loved in return. It was trying to make me aware that I need to give reign to the softer, more feminine aspects of my personality at times, and not always be the strong, silent, masculine type.

On a spiritual level, it was showing me that it can work with me to help me access my highest levels of consciousness and self-awareness, improving my powers of introspection, reflection and perception.

Crystal: Obsidian

Origin – Igneous

Colour –Light blue

Generally held characteristics

Obsidian is molten lava which has cooled so rapidly that it has had no time for crystalline structures to form. The result is 'volcanic glass.' Blue obsidian has an affinity with the throat chakra and can be used to enhance communication. It is also believed to facilitate and enhance out of body experiences (astral travel) and telepathy.

Physically, it aids speech problems, disorders of the eyes, mental deterioration, and also relieves pain. Overall, it can be used to open the aura so that healing can be received energetically through the physical body.

Attunement message

When I asked for the properties of this crystal I was told, 'The crystal is clear. It turns everything upside down.' The world then turned upside down.

The first thing I saw was a window, which was open. Then myself as a child in my school uniform, looking out of the living room window, happy and innocent. Dad was taking me to school. Mum was very much in the background. I kept looking for her in the house but I couldn't find her. She was like a memory.

Then it flashed to the present day – Dad and I (both adults), hugging in the hall and crying. The reality of Mum being dead but also the feeling of being lucky enough to have had a good, dedicated Mum during my childhood and adulthood up until now. Realisation.

Next I saw a black bat or vampire on a magenta backdrop, flying upwards towards the moon. There was a feeling of clearing. Then I saw a white swan - purity and innocence floating down a river with dignity and grace but pedalling away like crazy below the surface in order to stay afloat. The swan flew up and turned into an angel. Healing. When I asked if there was anything else? I got the colour magenta and the words, 'calm, cleansing, and releasing.'

Interpretation

When you look through a blue obsidian crystal everything is turned upside down, which is what has happened to me recently with the death of my Mum. My world has been turned upside down! The image of me as child in my school uniform looking out the window with only my Dad around and no sign of my Mum is quite the opposite of how my childhood actually was. My mum was always there for me and she was the centre of my universe. Searching for her through the house like a memory is

83

reflective of what I do subconsciously each time I go home to N. Ireland. I walk around the house in and out of all the rooms, expecting to find her working in 'the bakery' at the back of the house.

The next scene is a recent one where I burst into tears in my Dad's arms after the reality sunk in and the realisation of the fact that Mum isn't there, well at least not in the physical sense. I do realise how lucky I am to have had such a wonderful, dedicated and loving mother who was always there for me throughout my childhood, teenage years, and adulthood, up until New Year.

The black bat/vampire are scary images flying away, drawing lifeblood, life-force energy, and are perhaps representative of my fear of having lost such a key person from my life. The feeling of clearing is probably just that negativity lifting off. The white swan is how I feel sometimes, doing everything I can to put a brave face on things and hold things together, whilst feeling emotionally traumatised and terrified inside/below the surface. The swan flew up and turned into an angel and I got the word 'healing', perhaps indicating that when I open up to receive healing and release/let go of these emotions I will be able to heal internally and therefore be able to 'fly.'

The words 'calm, cleansing, releasing' suggest that this would be an excellent stone for helping me to remain calm, whilst releasing these feelings/emotions and cleansing, rebalancing and healing me.

Crystal: Petalite

Origin – Igneous

Colour – Pale pink

Generally held characteristics

Sometimes referred to as 'the stone of the angels', petalite can be used to promote and enhance connection to the angelic realms and also to enhance psychic abilities. Pink petalite has an affinity to the heart chakra and can be used to gently release and clear emotional baggage.

On the physical level, it alleviates pain and can benefit the lungs, muscular and skeletal systems.

Attunement message

When I asked to be shown the special properties of this crystal, I was told, 'ascension, high energy and strong vibrations.' I felt a swallowing sensation in my throat followed by coughing and clearing. The words 'release from the web' came to mind, and I saw a dragonfly which then became a beautiful butterfly. This was followed by a lovely magenta colour. When I asked if there was anything else, I got a real sense that the crystal will enhance clairaudience and clairsentience.

Interpretation

This attunement was very straightforward and to the point. Once again, as expected with a crown chakra crystal, this was a very fast, high energy and strong vibrational attunement. The swallowing in the throat and coughing was clearing and opening the throat chakra to allow links to spiritual vibrations. The higher chakras 8-12 are accessed through the throat chakra.

Clearing and releasing, as has happened in many of my other attunements, was symbolised by nature and synonymous with flying. The feeling of being released from a web symbolised the release/freedom from a trap or blockage.

The dragonfly, which changed into a beautiful butterfly, was a wonderful visual analogy of the Kundalini energy being activated, releasing blockages and replenishing all of my chakras, as represented by the colours of the butterfly. I think it also symbolised how this crystal could be used by myself, or with others, for releasing blockages in order to facilitate links to high spiritual growth and development.

Crystal: *Rose Quartz Merkabah Star*

Origin – Igneous

Colour – Pink

Generally held characteristics

The Merkabah: Mer = Light, Ka = Spirit, Ba = Body

The shape of this crystal is two tetrahedrons interlocked to form a three-dimensional Star of David. It is a powerful tool for shifting patterns in the DNA and also psychological patterns and the beliefs on which they are based. It brings balance and harmony, and is useful in stressful situations due to its ability to align the physical, emotional, mental and spiritual bodies.

Attunement message

The properties revealed to me were, 'magical, mystical.'

The first thing I saw was a white unicorn flying upwards. Next, a silhouette of a white horse on a red background. This was followed by a North American Indian Totem pole and then I saw the white horse again. I felt a surging of energy through my heart chakra and I had a sense of swallowing in my throat. Then I started coughing. It was very fast acting, and my attunement finished quickly.

Interpretation

I loved this attunement although it was short and finished quickly because of the very fast acting energies involved. A Merkabah Star is sometimes called the 'Chariot of the Soul' because it connects us to our higher selves. This is extremely relevant for me as a white unicorn symbolises an elevated state of consciousness representative of a stimulated crown chakra. The white horse on a red background is the Light energy of spirituality and the red is reflective of the grounding, earthly energies of reality, indicating the crystal's ability to align the mind, body and spirit.

The surging of energy through the heart chakra shows the energy surge when integrating the heart and the crown. I think this was also stronger because the crystal I chose was a pink Rose Quartz Merkabah Star, the colour of which has an affinity to the heart chakra. Once again there was a clearing in the throat chakra, as indicated by the swallowing and coughing. This was probably a release of suppressed emotions as I have been continuing to suppress my grief following my Mum's death. A lot of my attunements have shown me that when I release/let go of my blockages and fears, then my personal growth will accelerate allowing me to fulfil my ambitions.

Crystal: Ruby in Zoisite

Origin – Metamorphic

Colour – Green/red with black inclusions

Generally held characteristics

Zoisite encourages recovery after illness or acute stress. It is extremely good at transmuting negative energy, bringing joy, enthusiasm and courage to deal with all life issues. Physically, this stone helps with diseases of the testicles and ovaries, stimulating fertility and potency.

Attunement message

I visualised the Island of Staffa off the West Coast of Scotland with crashing waves, and heard the music 'Fingal's Cave' by Mendelssohn. Almost immediately, the visualisation changed and I saw the Island of Iona where all was peace and calm. A dove flew overhead with an olive branch in its beak. I asked the crystal Deva, 'how can I work with this crystal?' Immediately, I visualised soaring, crashing waves and heard triumphant music. The visualisation changed and I was on a deserted beach looking out over a wide, flat sea. I looked about me and suddenly realised that I was no longer on the beach but I was in Iona Abbey, listening to the soothing chants of the monks. I felt spiritually at peace, and was aware of an immense sense of inner calm.

Interpretation

This crystal was showing me how it could form a link between the lower and higher levels of consciousness, bringing me to a deeper knowledge and understanding of my personal potential. It can help me to achieve the perfect state of love and harmony, restoring my faith and confidence in the Divine Plan.

Crystal: Rutilated Quartz

Origin – Igneous

Colour – Clear, with golden rutile

Generally held characteristics

This crystal can be used to cleanse and energise the morphogenic field (the aura), thus bringing light and lightness on all levels. It is helpful in difficult situations where there is a need to break free from unhelpful relationships or associations, and has a mood-lifting effect.

It is useful in cases of chronic conditions of exhaustion and problems of the respiratory tract.

Attunement message

Initially, I saw a canoe sailing along in still water, where the only movement was of two arms which became the paddles. The scene then changed to a green blob, which became an open green eye, which blinked. I then saw waltzing waters, as if through a veil or curtain as the water danced. This was followed by the sight of a bright golden ball, which reminded me of the sun and golden energy radiating.

Interpretation

I believe that this crystal was showing me that I am in control. I am the canoe and my arms are taking me forward. It is a crystal that can be associated with the solar plexus chakra, the centre of our personal will, power and control.

Rutilated quartz belongs to the tetragonal system which has an affinity with the heart chakra. I think that this is the reason why the eye that I saw was green, one of the colours of the heart chakra, with the third eye also being closely linked with the solar plexus. The eye opens and blinks to let me know that the third eye *is* open, confirming to me that I need to let go of my insecurities and to accept and trust my intuition.

The waltzing waters reminded me of the waltzing waters at Newtonmore, near Aviemore. They were very beautiful and colourful to watch. With the veil distorting my view, I feel that the crystal was showing me that I am not realising my full potential.

I think that this is a crystal which will help me let go and support me as I move forward in life. In nature, the sun provides energy to make things grow, and also lifts our mood. It is, I believe, a crystal to support my spiritual growth and development.

Crystal: Selenite

Origin – Sedimentary

Colour – White

Generally held characteristics

Selenite is a form of crystallized gypsum. It brings clarity of mind, accesses angelic consciousness and reaches past and future lives. Physically, it is an excellent stone for aligning the spinal column, promoting flexibility in the muscular structure and for re-energising the body.

Attunement message

Before I sat down to attune to this crystal, I had had a particularly tiring day, feeling drained of energy and experiencing some discomfort around my recent operation scar tissue. On attuning to the crystal I immediately experienced a tremendous surge of warm, white energy entering my crown chakra. The energy progressed downwards through the chakras until it reached the sacral chakra. I visualised the swathes of pure white energy surrounding the scar tissue and I felt my insides grow increasingly warmer.

Interpretation

The crystal was telling me that I should have listened to my body earlier and recognised its need to rest and re-charge. It was showing me how it can help us to make time to relax and also how it can re-energise the physical body when it is suffering from exhaustion.

This will be a good crystal to use when I have pushed my body to its physical limits and am feeling completely worn out and depleted of energy.

Crystal: Smoky Quartz Generator

Origin – Igneous:

Colour – Brown

Generally held characteristics

It is generally accepted that smoky quartz stimulates the base chakra and grounds and protects us. It has the ability to absorb and transform negative emotions and energy patterns, encouraging positive attitudes by dissolving the anger and resentment which cause dis-ease. It can be used to strengthen the adrenal glands, kidneys and pancreas as well as for pain-relief, relaxation and aiding depression. Because it grounds and stimulates our higher awareness, it is also an excellent stone for meditation.

Attunement message

When first attuning to this crystal I visualised bright white light around my head. Immediately, the colour changed to reddish/orange with a brown/black 'blob' at the bottom. At first I could not understand what this was. Then I saw twisted, ugly brown/black faces and knew that the crystal was showing me my 'shadow side.' I felt movement around my base, sacral and solar plexus chakras and the visualisation ended.

Interpretation

This crystal was showing me that it could help me to recognise and acknowledge the negative traits of my lower-self personalities – the times when I am the rescuer, the persecutor or the victim. The bright white light suggested that these could be transformed into positive expression. The colour change to reddish/orange with a brown/black 'blob' suggests stored up anger, resentment or aggression. Working with this crystal can therefore help me to allow these deep-rooted feelings to surface, to acknowledge them and to discover how I might transform them into more constructive and affirmative expressions.

Crystal: Star Rose Quartz

Origin – Igneous

Colour – Pink

Generally held characteristics

Rose quartz promotes self-love, calmness and clarity by gently restoring balance and harmony. It heals grief and other emotional traumas and is therefore a master healer of the emotional body. It dissolves self-criticism and self-judgement and allows us to acknowledge and show our emotions. It teaches unconditional love both of ourselves and others. It balances yin/yang energies and can be used to detoxify the whole body, especially the kidneys, adrenal glands, reproductive imbalances and chest problems when placed on the thymus.

Star Rose Quartz possesses all of these qualities. In addition, it activates the Divine purpose and teaches us that unlimited love should be easy to use, and that to do this we have to allow ourselves to be vulnerable. Star Rose Quartz helps us to focus and find the strength in vulnerability.

Attunement message

I visualised myself at the centre of the Star Rose Quartz crystal. The sphere was made of ice crystals that I had surrounded myself with, effectively shutting myself off from contact with others and preventing the giving/receiving of love. Shafts of bright light started to radiate from around about me at the centre of the sphere and caused the ice to shatter, so freeing me. I felt physically and emotionally lighter around the heart and solar plexus areas.

Interpretation

The crystal was showing me that I am the co-creator of my own destiny, because I am the one who is putting up the barriers of control between myself and others. Hence the feeling of lightness as tension was released, after the attunement, in the solar plexus region – our centre of will and power.

It was telling me that it can work with me to break down these barriers and let unconditional love into my life, by teaching me that it is safe to be vulnerable because only by doing this can I learn to love both myself and others.

Crystal: Sunstone

Origin – Igneous

Colour – Deep yellow

Generally held characteristics

Despite its name, sunstone comes in a range of colours as well as yellow. It is an iridescent feldspar that owes its appearance to the presence of microscopically thin hematite or goethite platelets. This crystal can be used to both clear and energise the solar plexus chakra, dissolving stress and bringing increased vitality. In ancient Greece it was thought to represent the Sun God, bringing abundance to those fortunate enough to wear or carry it.

Physically, it can be used to dissolve tension in the stomach and to relieve ulcers. It is also believed to be useful for stimulating the autonomous nervous system and for stimulating self-healing.

Attunement message

I visualised myself walking in the edge of the water on a deserted tropical beach. I could hear the water lapping on the shore and I noticed that there were palm trees waving gently in the breeze. A turtle appeared out of the water and crawled onto the beach. It looked up at me and seemed to be asking for help because it was 'beached' and needed to get back into the water. I turned it around and dragged it to the water, watching it swim away to safety. A truck appeared on the beach and soldiers with guns jumped out. I knew instinctively that they were looking for the turtle, and when they found nothing they got back into the truck and drove away. I remember thinking that it was lucky that I came along when I did, and I felt happy that I had helped the turtle to escape because I knew they would have killed it.

Interpretation

The crystal was showing me that it can help us to be in tune with our instincts, bringing us the knowledge that we will be in the right place at the right time. It will be a good crystal to use when we are feeling threatened or under attack in some way, because it will help us to know instinctively what action is needed in the circumstances.

Crystal: Tanzanite

Origin –Metamorphic

Colour – Purple

Generally held characteristics

A variety of zoisite, this crystal enhances communication on all levels, awakening the higher self by breaking through the limitations of third dimensional thinking. A truly amazing stone, it will link us with our Soul, the Divine Plan and reveal our true purpose in this lifetime.

A metamorphic crystal, tanzanite is an excellent stone to use when we are undergoing change or transition, or are experiencing a crisis. Its colour is purple, and it is therefore particularly useful for opening and balancing the third eye chakra. It will help those who are ready to receive and work with its energy to become aware of the connection to their own true essence. It will provide answers to the questions, 'who am I?' and 'what is my purpose in life?' It is an excellent stone for opening and developing spiritual awareness.

In addition, it possesses all the qualities also described for zoisite.

Attunement message

I visualised myself in a small temple at the top of the pyramid, El Castillo, in Chichen Itza, Mexico. I was regally dressed, and my face was being painted with beautiful blue and gold paint. A head-dress of the same colours was being placed on my head. I was led out onto the ledge surrounding the temple and saw a High Priest waiting for me there. Crowds of people knelt on the ground below the pyramid. The priest pushed me onto a sword which pierced my body, straight through the heart and out of my back. Immediately, I watched myself standing at the edge of the pyramid and jumping off, spreading my arms which were covered with a cloak of white feathers. I saw myself flying off into a bright, white shining light high in the sky. I felt no pain, only a sense of peace, calm and freedom. However, as the visualisation faded, the words 'who am I?' came into my mind, followed by a feeling of sadness and a deep sense of being unconnected to the true essence of myself.

Interpretation

This visualisation related to an experience I had in 2001, when standing at the top of the Mayan pyramid El Castillo in Chichen Itza. I had felt compelled to go to the edge of the pyramid and jump off – yet I felt no fear at the prospect.

The crystal was showing me a past life in which I had been sacrificed – not by being thrown off the pyramid, but by being made to fall onto a sword, which pierced my heart. This symbolism of emotional pain has since caused me to ask myself, 'is this why I find it so hard to be open and loving of myself and others?'

At the point of death, the crystal showed me that my soul had left my body and soared up into the sky. This was clearly telling me that it can help me to connect to my higher self and to the very essence of who I am – symbolised by the soaring of my soul into the sky and the words 'who am I?'

The sense of disconnectedness suggested that I needed to work further with the crystal – which I did later that same day.

Second attunement message

The words 'who am I?' from the previous attunement were visualised. 'Heart Healer' and 'Mender of Hearts' came to mind. I saw a human heart, frozen in ice, being melted by a blowtorch. I saw a green, beating heart surrounded by purple light and I knew that this was a representation of my life-path. I know and understand that often the cause of dis-ease stems from emotional (heart) problems, and I also know that the crystal was showing me that events occurring throughout my own emotionally traumatic life have been part of the learning process to prepare me for this current phase of my life.

Crystal: Topaz

Origin – Igneous

Colour – Pale blue

Generally held characteristics

Topaz encourages self-realisation and the shaping of our lives according to our own wishes. By stimulating the throat chakra, blue topaz facilitates spiritual development, thereby opening us up to our own inner wisdom. It also helps us to see the bigger picture by clarifying our focus and intentions.

Attunement message

The fingers of both hands started to tingle (it felt like a million tiny bubbles bursting in my hands!) and I visualised myself sitting on the beach at Scalpsie Bay, a place I know and love on the Isle of Bute. I saw seals playing in the water and felt the warm sun on my face. The words 'space' and 'tranquillity' came into my mind.

Interpretation

This crystal was showing me that it can be used to bring us peace and spirituality by encouraging a calm and contemplative view of life. In so doing, we are able to relax and focus on our inner wisdom, by opening up and being ready to connect with our higher levels of consciousness and wisdom.

Crystal: Topaz

Origin – Igneous

Colour – Champagne

Generally held characteristics

Topaz is an excellent crystal for encouraging self-confidence and self-belief. It makes us aware of our true abilities and knowledge, and assists in shaping our lives according to our own wishes, rather than the wishes of others.

Physically, it can be used to strengthen the nervous and digestive systems and to stimulate the metabolism.

Attunement message

I was told that the properties of this crystal are, ' cleansing, balancing, and control of my own life'. I got some very vivid colours - orange, red, and magenta. Then I was riding on a horse, bareback. It was a chestnut, and had no bridle. I felt free and had complete freedom to go where I wanted and to do anything I wanted to. I was asked 'who is in control?' and was told 'take back control of your own life.' Next I saw purple, which was very bright. This was followed by a spider's web. I heard, 'release yourself!' Then I saw yellow. I felt a change in body temperature and I went slightly colder.

Interpretation

There was no black / grey in this attunement. I moved through some colours – orange, red, bright pink, yellow, purple. This was probably symbolic of a clearing/cleansing of my chakras. The horse was very interesting and I believe the message there was for me to take control of my own life.

Although I was not in a relationship when I did this attunement, I did not feel like I was completely in control of my own life as I was being heavily influenced, and to some degree 'controlled' by an ex-boyfriend and another friend. I have since taken back control and am now in the driving seat again.

The yellow colour is linked to the solar plexus, the centre of our emotions, joy and happiness. I think this is indicating that when I take back control I will be happier, more secure and have increased self-esteem. Yellow is also linked to mental ability, to logic and reasoning and our ability to digest situations and information.

Crystal: Tourmaline Quartz

Origin – Igneous

Colour – Clear quartz with black tourmaline rutiles

Generally held characteristics

Tourmaline comes in many colours, the energy of each colour relates to each of the seven chakras. It clears and stimulates each of the energy centres of the body, balances male/female energies and promotes personal growth and transformation.

Tourmaline cuts through negativity, bringing light to the body and the clarity to go forward with confidence. It brings focus and objectivity and allows us to align with the Divine Blueprint to discover our purpose in life. It teaches us how to create our own reality by exploring our own purpose and will, and our own higher and lower self.

On the cellular level, tourmaline facilitates the transformation of our DNA structure and nervous systems, and changes our hormonal secretions to bring our bodily systems into balance.

Tourmaline quartz is clear quartz with black tourmaline rutiles inside, and so combines the qualities of both of these crystals.

Attunement message

When I held and observed this crystal I felt a tingling, pulsating energy in my hand and I noticed that the crystal appeared to puff out and expand. The cloudy parts of the quartz seemed to grow more dense and the rutiles looked more prominent. When I held it to the base chakra and asked to meet the crystal Deva, I saw her as an old woman dressed in a long, black hooded cloak, walking through a cold, snowy wasteland carrying a black staff. She beckoned me to follow, and as I did so I saw her throw off her cloak and transform into a young, golden-haired woman wearing a long, vivid blue dress.

The scenery changed too. Gone was the snow and cold, and in their place was a woodland bathed in bright white light. Small bluebirds sang and flew from tree to tree. Her black staff became a wand which, when she waved it in the air, left behind hundreds of glittering clear crystals.

Interpretation

The Deva was showing me that this crystal will be my personal tool of transformation. It will help me to recognise and to utilise my innate strength and courage so that I can release all the negative things in my life that are holding me back and that I have now outgrown. It will help me to transform, develop and move on to achieve what I was meant to do in this life, also helping me to make the transition into higher levels of consciousness. It will clarify my purpose and my vision, bringing extreme light and energy, while at the same time keeping me balanced and grounded.

Crystal: Tourmaline

Origin – Igneous

Colour - Pink

Generally held characteristics

In addition to the characteristics already stated for tourmaline, pink tourmaline promotes extroversion and sociability. Physically, it aids blood circulation and the functioning of the spleen and liver.

Attunement message

I visualised a powerful white horse galloping at great speed, mane flying. The horse grew wings and flew off into the distance. The scene changed to a green field covered in masses of purple flowers. I felt an immense sense of calm and peace.

Interpretation

Through the symbolism of the white horse, this crystal was showing me that it can help me to let go, instead of always trying to rationalise situations.

As for the green field and purple flowers, the colour green symbolises growth and purple is a colour associated with intuition. This suggests that I should trust my higher self and my intuition – they will give me all the guidance I need to help me handle any situation and to make the right decisions.

Crystal: Turquoise (African)

Origin – Sedimentary

Colour – Turquoise/green

Generally held characteristics

A protective crystal, turquoise was once used as an amulet in the breastplate of the High Priest in ancient civilisations. It protects from external influences and bestows a calm yet cheerful energy. Also, it is believed to promote and stimulate romantic love, helping us to recognise what makes us happy and unhappy.

Turquoise strengthens the physical body and aids exhaustion, viral infections, and the eyes. It is detoxifying and anti-inflammatory.

Attunement message

This attunement started with bright orange. Then a black dot appeared and fell from the top to the bottom. Lots of colours next – orange, red, violet, and blue. My throat was burning and it felt like it was on fire. I was being shown that the healing properties of this crystal aid the glands, clearing blockages and balancing the thyroid.

This attunement had a mystical, magical feeling. I visualised a bright orange African sunset, which reminded me of Kenya. This was followed by a gorgeous blue. Then orange again with a path winding through it. I asked, 'is this symbolising my path and am I on the correct path?' I saw what resembled a split, but felt reassured that I had chosen correctly and that everything would work out in the end.

Next I had a feeling of being on Safari. I saw a giraffe and then the scene jumped to a glorious beach. It was paradise-like, with white sand and crystal clear sea. There was a wedding scene and the groom had his trousers rolled up, paddling in the sea. I had an overwhelming feeling of happiness, and joy.

Last, lots of travelling and flashes of different places or sites – mountains, architecture etc.

Afterwards I felt happy, calm, relaxed, almost mystical.

Interpretation

This was a fabulous attunement. I really enjoyed it and felt a rush of excitement and enthusiasm. This is not surprising as orange represents joy, warmth, radiance and well-being. The black dot falling away was like a clearing or letting go before the excitement and adventure could truly begin. I moved through a wide variety of colours, which was probably a rebalancing of my energy. This ended with blue, the throat chakra colour, which was also reflected by the burning sensation there. The fact that this crystal can be used for glands, clearing blockages and the thyroid is appropriate as I have a problem with my pituitary gland being out of balance and my thyroid is underactive.

The African influence on this attunement must be to do with the fact that it was an African Turquoise. I felt reassured that I am on the right path and that I will be guided through any decisions I have to make in the future. I think the split represents the decision that I had to make fairly recently about whether or not to get back together with my ex-boyfriend (after twelve months of being split up). I feel that this crystal was reassuring me that I had made the right decision in staying friends but not getting back together as a couple. As for the travelling, well I hope it is an indication of things to come! I have recently discovered, since the attunement, that turquoise is known as 'the stone of travellers', and is frequently carried as an amulet when travelling. This attunement would confirm this.

Further Interpretation and understanding (2010):

My ex-boyfriend and I remained good friends and gradually spent more and more time together. After eighteen months of being split up we finally got back together. I believe that the fact we remained split up for a longer period of time made us realise just how much we loved and missed one another. Despite having being together for years before the split there was no talk of marriage or long-term commitment and yet within a couple of months of us getting back together we got engaged and were married six months later. Our wedding day was the happiest day of our lives. We celebrated the day with immediate family and close friends and the air was filled with happiness and joy, just like the attunement had predicted. Whilst we didn't paddle in the sea on that day we certainly did when we went on honeymoon to Majorca, where we travelled around the island to various different places admiring the gorgeous scenery, beaches, mountain ranges and architectural heritage.

Sometimes I look back with sadness at the fact we ever split up at all, but we both realise that it was part of our journey. It played an important part in helping us to appreciate each other and, strange as it may seem, it actually brought us closer together and our relationship is much stronger as a result.

7: The Significance of Sacred Geometry

Historical Perspective

In ancient time, architects, designers and builders used sacred geometry as a tool to design temples and pyramids in accordance with cosmic patterns and universal truths. In doing so they created some of the most beautiful and astonishing works of art which are in perfect harmony with their natural surroundings. Some obvious examples are the pyramids of Egypt, the Parthenon in Greece and the Gothic cathedrals across Europe. In the Western world, from Greek times until the end of the Renaissance, the ancient arts of arithmetic, geometry, music and astronomy were studied and practised as sacred disciplines. They were known as the *quadrivium* or 'Four Ways.' Today they are sometimes better known with different names. *Numerology* – the spiritual science of number; *sacred geometry* – the spiritual science of form; *harmonics* – the spiritual science of dimension, relationship and proportion of music and *calendrics* – the spiritual science of the cycles of time.

The word 'geometry' is derived from the Greek *geometria,* meaning 'earth measurement' (*geo* means *earth* and *metron* means *measurement*). This stems from the ancient origins of geometry when it was used to lay out patterns on the earth in order to measure fields and establish ground plans for sacred structures. At this time, all geometry was sacred – for two reasons.

113

First, the Earth itself was believed and understood to be a living and holy being, and those who measured it recognized their responsibilities as mediators between the Earth and the people. There is plenty of evidence that this was so in the sacred status of standing stones, stone circles and boundary stones and in the rituals that were performed at the founding of a city or the building of a temple.

Second, it was recognized early on that geometry itself offered pathways into the subtle realm of meaning and spirit that we call *sacred.* Mastery of the laws of geometric form provided individuals with the tools to reshape the world not only on the physical level – but on subtler levels as well.

The principles of sacred geometry can equally be applied to the design of a stone circle, the erection of a new cathedral, the proportions of a Renaissance painting – all require the same geometrical principles of balance and harmony – the need to join geometric theory with creative expression. As a result, we are still able to see today some of the most amazing and beautiful structures which were created using these principles.

Sacred Geometry – what is it?

Sacred geometry can be defined as 'the art of transmitting divine wisdom through the symbolic use of geometric forms.' It is based on the belief that certain knowledge was so divine that it was thought necessary to create a cipher available only to the initiated in order to prevent it being made known to the uninitiated.

In the 1980s, Professor Robert Moon, University of Chicago, demonstrated that the entire Periodic Table of Elements (quite literally, everything in the physical world) is based on five geometric forms - The Platonic Solids.

The Platonic solids

The platonic solids are a group of five three-dimensional solid shapes, each containing all congruent angles and sides. Also, if circumscribed with a sphere, all vertexes would touch the edge of the sphere. It was Euclid who would later prove in his book, entitled 'The Elements', that these are the only five shapes which actually fit this criteria.

They represent a blueprint for all the cell structures in the bodies of humans, animals, plants and minerals. They were first named *Platonic Solids* by Plato, a contemporary of ancient geometricians, who visualised the world as being composed of basic elements – each representing a particular shape. Plato expressed each of these shapes as 'solids' – the basic building blocks for all life forms.

In his book, *Timaeus*, written in approximately 350 BC, Plato first described these solids, linking them to different elements of reality. The *tetrahedron,* containing four sides, and actually found twice within Metatron's cube (the star tetrahedron is a combination of two tetrahedrons), is used to represent Fire.

The *cube,* containing six sides, and also found twice within Metatron's cube, represents the Earth. The *octahedron,* containing eight sides, represents the Air. The *icosahedron,* containing twenty sides, represents the Water. Finally, the *dodecahedron,* containing twelve sides, is used to represent the Cosmos.

Music and Geometry

The discovery of the relationship of geometry and mathematics to music within the Classical Period is attributed to Pythagoras, who found that a string stopped halfway along its length produced an octave, while a ratio of 3/2 produced a fifth interval and 4/3 produced a fourth. Pythagoreans believed that this gave music powers of healing, as it could 'harmonise' the out-of-balance body, and this belief has been revived in modern times. Hans Jenny, a physician who pioneered the study of geometric figures formed by wave interactions and named the study *cymatics,* is often cited in this context. However, Dr Jenny did not make healing claims for his work.

Even though Hans Jenny did pioneer *cymatics* in modern times, the study of geometric relationships to wave interaction (sound) obviously has much older roots (Pythagoras). A work that shows ancient peoples' understanding of sacred geometry can be found in Scotland. In the Rosslyn Chapel, Thomas J. Mitchell, found what he calls 'frozen music.' Apparently, there are 213 cubes with different symbols that are believed to have musical significance. After twenty seven years of study and research, Mitchell has found the correct pitches and tonality that matches each symbol on each cube, revealing harmonic and melodic progressions. He has fully discovered the 'frozen music', which he has named the Rosslyn Motet.

The Fibonacci Sequence

Leonardo Fibonacci was an Italian mathematician born c. 1170, whose introduction to Europe popularized the Hindu-Arabic number system (also called the decimal system). He contributed significantly to number theory, and during his life published several important texts. He is perhaps best known for the Fibonacci numbers or sequence, a numerical series found most frequently in the natural world.

The Fibonacci sequence is generated by adding the previous two numbers in the list together to form the next number, and so on. (1, 1, 2, 3, 5, 8, 13, 21, 34, 55 etc.). Furthermore, if you divide any number in the Fibonacci sequence by the previous number, for example 55 divided by 34, or 21 divided by 13, the answer is always close to 1.61803. This number is known as the *golden ratio.*

There are clear examples of sacred geometry (and golden mean geometry) to be found in nature and matter. Some of these are:

- All types of crystal, natural and manufactured
- The hexagonal geometry of snowflakes
- Creatures exhibiting spiral patterns: e.g. snails, and some shellfish
- Birds and flying insects which exhibit clear golden mean proportions in their bodies and wings
- The geometric atomic patterns that all solid metals exhibit
- The Great Pyramid at Giza – the height of this pyramid is in Phi ratio (the golden mean ratio) to its base.
- Deoxyribonucleic Acid (DNA) – contains the coded information which is necessary for the development and function of all living organisms (except RNA viruses). DNA consists of two intertwined vertical helixes. The length of the curve in each of these helixes is thirty four angstroms and the width is twenty one angstroms. One angstrom is one hundred millionth of a centimetre. The numbers 21 and 34 are two consecutive numbers in the Fibonacci sequence.

The Golden Ratio

The golden ratio, also known as the god ratio, golden proportion, golden mean, golden section, golden number, divine proportion or sectio divina, is an irrational number, approximately 1.618 033 988 749 894 848, that possesses many interesting properties. Shapes proportioned according to the golden ratio have long been considered aesthetically pleasing in Western cultures, and the golden ratio is still used frequently in art and design, suggesting a natural balance between symmetry and asymmetry. The ancient Pythagoreans, who defined numbers as expressions of ratios (and not as units as is common today), believed that reality is numerical and that the golden ratio expressed an underlying truth about existence. Artists, scientists and designers take the human body, the proportions of which are set out according to the golden ratio, as their measure. Most famously, Leonardo da Vinci used the golden ratio in setting out the proportions of the human body.

The significance and use of sacred geometry in healing

Geometry in nature arranges the shapes of the molecules and crystals that make up our bodies and the physical cosmos - from the spirals of the nautilus shell, the centre of a sunflower to the hexagonal symmetry of snowflakes and the honeycomb in a beehive.

119

These inevitably follow geometrical archetypes, which reveal to us the nature of each form and its vibrational resonances. They are also symbolic of the underlying metaphysical principle of the inseparable relationship of the part to the whole. This principle of interconnectedness, inseparability and union provides us with a continuous reminder of our relationship to the whole.

Western scientific thinking now accepts the importance of pattern and proportional relationships between particles – together with the notion that it is these relationships rather than the particles themselves which affect our perception of the world.

When we become ill or there is dis-ease on whatever level it is because our *subtle energy patterns* have been disturbed or disrupted and we no longer vibrate at a level which ensures our optimum health and well-being. Placing appropriate crystals on the chakras or in the aura assists in realigning the energy of our physical body with that of the subtle bodies.

In addition, it is possible to enhance or influence the energy of individual crystals by the use of an appropriate *crystal grid* to create an energy network which will support the healing process. Having some basic knowledge of the shapes used in sacred geometry, together with their esoteric meanings, provides us with a useful tool which we can draw on to safely and effectively to support a healing session, or to change the energy in a particular space or place.

Crystal Grids

The Circle

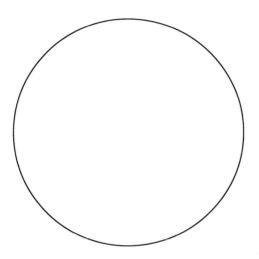

In sacred geometry the circle is a symbol of unity, oneness, continuity and potential. It represents the ever-turning heavens and spirit.

It is a useful grid to use when there is a need to create *flow* and *harmony*. For example, when individuals need encouragement to 'tell their story' – or in a group situation, to stimulate discussion and exchange of ideas. The circle is *not useful* in situations which require decision-making.

Suggested crystals:

Amethyst – cleanses the atmosphere of tension and negativity

Clear quartz – stimulates creativity, new ideas and a desire for action

Rose quartz – provides a safe, loving space to facilitate change. Useful for self-help groups such as drugs counselling, AA etc.

Note: *For all grids, different crystals will bring different energy networks.*

The Spiral

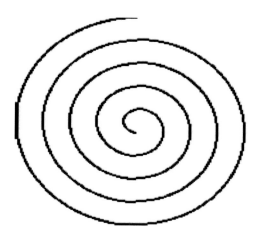

This is one of the most ancient patterns in sacred geometry. It symbolises the unfolding of what is hidden.

It can be useful when someone has difficulty in seeing what needs to be let go of, helping them to a clearer understanding of the need to release that which is no longer useful to them.

Suggested crystals:

Agate – aids self-analysis and perception of things that are hidden

Amethyst – brings mental focus and aids decision-making

Lapis Lazuli – clarifies the mind and encourages objectivity

The Square

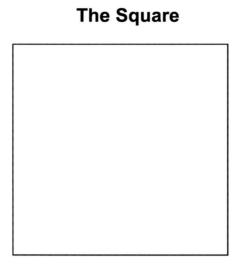

In sacred geometry, the square represents the Earth and matter and so is a symbol of stability, protection, reality and of being grounded,

It can be useful in situations where a person is feeling scattered, confused or is finding it too difficult to cope with life. Its energy is restrictive and confining, offering little room for movement and provides them with a safe place to 'just be.' The square is *not useful* in situations which require movement.

Suggested crystals:

Black tourmaline – clears negativity, reduces stress and tension

Smoky quartz – reduces stress and tension

The Cross

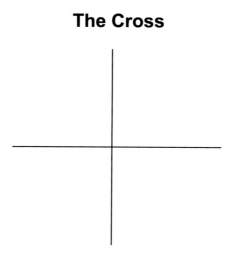

A symbol of union, the cross unites the material with the spirit world. It represents intersection and interaction – the crossing of two lines at right angles suggests a crossroads with potential options and choices about direction.

It can be useful in situations where an individual is faced with endings and new beginnings, and can help them to see with clarity the relevance and potential consequences of the opportunities being presented.

Suggested crystals:

Blue-green jade – encourages reflection and patience, and helps to dispel feelings of being overwhelmed and not in control

Chiastolite – sometimes known as 'the cross stone', it aids analysis of a situation and supports when making the transition from one circumstance to another

The Equilateral Triangle

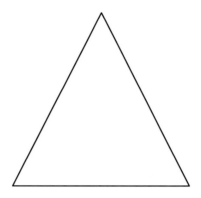

Having all three sides of equal length, this shape symbolises rigidity and stability, together with the possibility of growth and expansion suggested by the uppermost apex.

It can be useful when someone needs to adopt a more orderly and structured approach to help them realise their full potential. When faced with failure - this grid helps to support the manifestation of personal wishes, hopes and aspirations into solid reality.

Suggested crystals:

Fluorite – stimulates mentally, helping with the organization and rapid processing of information

Leopardskin jasper – brings balance between passivity and activity while supporting the achievement of goals

Quadrature of the Circle

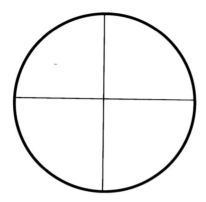

The division of the circle into four equal parts symbolises the world itself – the four directions, four seasons, the four symbolic elements of Earth, Wind, Fire and Water, and other esoteric fourfold patterns that shape our universe (in crystallography, the hexagonal system has four axes and is connected with our existence at the physical level). The presence of these patterns makes the quadrated circle a symbol of wholeness, integration and completion.

It is useful when someone is having difficulty seeing the 'whole picture' and is focussing only on the individual parts. This grid will help to bring balance, perspective and clarity of vision.

Suggested crystals:

Imperial topaz – expands the ability to think realistically and to generate ideas

The Hexagram (Star of David)

Formed from two equilateral triangles pointing in opposite directions, the hexagram symbolises 'as above, so below', the unity of opposites and the creation of harmony from conflict.

It can be useful in situations where a person is trying to find a balance between two opposing forces or is assuming that it is necessary to accept one and reject the other. The hexagram reminds us that it is not always necessary to choose between two alternatives, rather to recognise that both may have a valid place in our lives at certain times.

Suggested crystals:

Mookaite – encourages mental flexibility and the ability to evaluate several possibilities at the same time

The Octagram

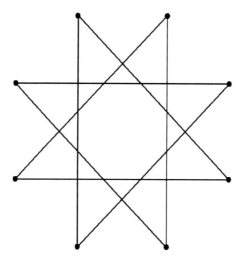

This eight-pointed star is formed from the interlacing of two squares and is a symbol of interaction between two established forces or factors. It represents wholeness through growth and regeneration.

It is useful in situations where there is a need to seek the help or guidance of another to bring something to completion. This may be the advice of a friend, a professional or may simply be seeking out relevant information to help resolve a situation. Asking for help can be a difficult task for some, and this grid promotes acceptance of the fact that in certain situations, it is necessary and appropriate to do so.

Suggested crystals:

Blue chalcedony – increases verbal communication and dissolves the fear of speaking out

Blue Siberian quartz – calms and lifts the spirits, aids communication

The Pentagram

This is one of the most controversial symbols in sacred geometry and is often associated with witches, pagans, mystics and magic. Magic is the primal form of power, and therefore it is no surprise that the pentagram symbolises all forms of power, together with the questions of ability and responsibility that power invokes. The number five is believed to represent the five metaphysical elements, reading clockwise from the topmost point these are, Spirit, Water, Fire, Earth and Air.

The pentagram grid can be useful in times of self-doubt or when there is a lack of confidence and the self-belief necessary to deal with a situation. This grid empowers individuals to take responsibility for and deal with the challenges they are currently facing.

Suggested crystals:

Astrophyllite – brings inspiration, perception and promotes the ability to achieve full potential

Garnet – supports during times of change and transition

8: The Future?

Rennison (2008) puts forward the belief that the Earth itself is undergoing transformation, and reports that Russian scientists believe that the Earth's frequency, which creates electromagnetic grid lines, is changing. When examined, the shape of the grid lines can be seen to contain crystal-like geometry and a diamond.

Further, she advocates that when we look at the Earth's core, where the Earth's magnetic field originates, the data suggests that the core is crystalline, exactly like an enormous diamond crystal about the size of our moon. Rennison stresses her belief that this diamond crystalline core is also a giant transmitter and receiver of energy and that we humans have the ability to transmit signals energetically to this receiver, which then transmits them out into the universe.

She reports that research by Washnis & Hricak (1993) suggests that the biogenic magnetite crystals, which can be found in a cluster of nerves in front of the pituitary and pineal glands, has led to the proposal that these glands may use information from the Earth's magnetic field to regulate the release of hormones in the human brain. Once released, these hormones directly control levels of conscious awareness and may, she suggests, act like tiny antennae which transmit and receive signals. Interestingly, she also notes that magnetite, the only natural magnet that can be found as a solid, is diamond-shaped, like an octahedron!

During his research, Gienger (1998) noticed that there was a distinct correlation between the crystal structure of minerals and the lifestyle of human beings. For example, when visiting the home of an acquaintance who was well-known for his exactness, self-discipline and correctness, he noticed that that he collected minerals – but only fluorite – which belong to the cubic system. He also observed that the same person used excessive amounts of salt to flavour his food (salt is a halide and also belongs to the cubic system). From this, Gienger was able to deduce that the inner structure of a mineral is mirrored in the way that people behave and live their lives. In this example, just as the cubic crystal system is characterized by a square, regular structure, the corresponding lifestyle is also characterized by order and control. 'A place for everything and everything in its place'.

Further research by Gienger confirmed these findings as he discovered that minerals with particular inner crystal systems were always chosen by people with particular traits. The more he observed people the more he came to understand that there were eight basic lifestyles which correspond to the seven crystal systems and the eighth amorphic state. He concluded that the reason for this lay in each individual's perception of their own reality and the strategy they have chosen for survival.

McTaggart (2009) believes that disease is scrambled or distorted information, and that information is simply patterns of energy. Fraser (2009) reports that researchers have learned how to stop this distortion and also that when this distortion is stopped the chemical and physiological processes begin to work correctly again. McTaggart goes on to say that if we can access the appropriate information then we can correct the scrambling. She also points out that this is exactly what new energy modalities are doing – correcting the information scrambling. This belief would seem to support the work of Gienger and his suggestion that using crystals of an appropriate structure can help to correct the distortion in the energy field.

It would appear that we are now on the threshold of a new understanding of how disease occurs, how information is transferred and how it is possible to enhance the transfer of information within living systems.

It is also becoming apparent that we are all part of a giant energy field and that it is the invisible stimuli in energy fields which govern the character of matter.

It is my belief that with this new understanding we are able to restore the body's repairing mechanism by using energy modalities such as crystals which utilises this understanding – thus providing a viable, scientific evidence-base for the use of crystals to enhance human health and well-being.

9: *Client Cases*

The following short selection of case résumés have been drawn from both private and nursing/residential home client cases since 2002. Names have been changed to protect client confidentiality.

Kevin's case

Kevin had been a drug addict for about nine years but has been 'clean' for the past three years. He'd heard about me from one of his friends, who was also a client, and she'd suggested that I might be able to help with his current concerns. At our meeting, Kevin explained that he had an important job interview and fitness test the following day about which he was not feeling confident. Also, he was worried that he wouldn't be fit enough to pass the test because of his previous addiction. He said that he didn't, understandably, want to take anything to 'calm his nerves' and had been told that crystals were non-invasive and might help him to feel more confident and less nervous.

Kevin's solar plexus and third eye chakras were out of balance at the emotional and mental levels respectively. I explained that the solar plexus is the centre of our gut feelings, personal will and power and that it is also the area most affected when we are stressed, nervous or anxious about anything. That's why people use the phrase 'butterflies in the stomach'. Also, that when the solar plexus is emotionally unbalanced there is often a knock-on effect to the third eye chakra with the result that our ability to think clearly and rationally is affected.

I chose to work with *yellow topaz* and *clear topaz* for the solar plexus and third eye chakras respectively. When the crystals were placed on the body Kevin immediately felt a rush of energy in the form of tingling and heat, and after a few minutes we could both hear gurgling from the solar plexus area as energy was being released.

Rationale for crystal choice

Topaz is an island silicate. One of the key properties of island silicates is the ability to strengthen self-belief and self-confidence. The colour yellow has an affinity with the solar plexus chakra and yellow topaz strengthens the nervous system. Clear topaz is able to clear all energy blocks.

After the crystals were removed, Kevin was smiling and appeared more relaxed, and he said that he felt easier in his mind about the interview and fitness test the following day.

Kevin 'phoned me the following week to say that he'd passed the fitness test with flying colours and that he'd got the job!

Margaret's case

Margaret was awaiting a date to go into hospital for an operation. She was feeling anxious and this had raised her blood pressure. She had requested a crystal layout for emotional calm and to lower her blood pressure so that she would be able to have the operation.

With the exception of the sacral, heart and crown chakras, all her energy centres were out of balance at the emotional level, confirming her emotional turmoil.

With this in mind, *petrified wood* was chosen for the base chakra, *yellow aragonite* for the solar plexus chakra, *blue fluorite* for the throat chakra and *lapis lazuli* for the third eye chakra.

While the crystals were on the body Margaret felt only a mild sensation of heat radiating from the base chakra up through the entire chakra system. I explained that this was the vibrational energy given off by the crystals and was being used to gently clear the blockages in her energy system.

Rationale for crystal choice

Petrified wood is fossilised wood which has been transformed into quartz. Belonging to the trigonal system and being of sedimentary formation, it is useful when there is a need to 'slow things down' and harmonise the subtle energies of the body. Its earthy brown colouring has an affinity with the base chakra – the centre for stability and security.

Yellow aragonite is emotionally calming to the solar plexus area, helping to release stress and anxiety. Essentially a carbonate, it has the energetic ability to stabilise processes that are proceeding too quickly.

Blue fluorite belongs to the cubic system and its gentle energy is emotionally stabilising. It is a halide and so has a dissolving property. The colour blue has an affinity with the throat chakra and is calming and soothing.

Lapis lazuli also belongs to the cubic system, the key feature of which is grounding and stabilising. It is a framework silicate and has a three-dimensional structure which gives it an absorbing effect. In this instance it was chosen to absorb heat and lower blood pressure.

Margaret returned the following week for a further session just two days before her operation. She told me that her blood pressure had been checked recently and that it was normal. Thankfully, her operation was a great success and she is now living a full and active life.

Deborah's case

Deborah had been diagnosed with irritable bowel syndrome (IBS) some months prior to our meeting. The symptoms were causing her distress and embarrassment, especially at work, and she was keen to know if there was anything I could do with the crystals to help her. During our initial discussion I discovered that she had had a poor relationship with her mother during her childhood. The basis of this was because no matter how well she did at school it was never enough. She was constantly being told by her mother that she should have worked harder and done better.

When I checked her energy system I found both the solar plexus and heart chakras to be profoundly out of balance at the emotional level. We had a long discussion about why this might be and she eventually acknowledged that she still felt angry and resentful towards her mother. I explained how holding on to deep-rooted feelings could be affecting her physically, because the health and well-being of the physical body can be influenced by the condition of the corresponding chakra. In her case, it was likely that the blockage in her solar plexus chakra (the area where we hold tension, stress, anger and anxiety) was having an influence on the corresponding physical part of her body, her digestive system. After discussion, she agreed to the use of appropriate crystals to help her start to release these deep-seated emotions. It was important to point out that the crystals selected might result in tears being shed, but that this was a normal part of the releasing process.

Deborah was OK with this and said that she felt that the time was right for her to start this process.

Yellow fluorite was chosen for the solar plexus chakra; *malachite* and *rose quartz* were chosen for the heart chakra.

Early in the session Deborah said that she felt bubbles rising from her stomach area, and also a heavy weight in the centre of her chest. At this point I gave her two rose quartz palm stones to hold – one for each hand – to encourage gentle energy release. (there are secondary chakras in the palms of the hands). As the session progressed she began to sigh heavily and somewhat shakily as energy was released, and eventually the tears began to flow, gently at first then accompanied by huge sobs. At this point we adjusted her position on the plinth to make her more comfortable, where she stayed until she was calm again.

Afterwards, we explored what had occurred during the release and she acknowledged that she felt a huge weight had been lifted from around her chest area.

Rationale for crystal choice

A halide, *yellow fluorite* has dissolving properties and was chosen to help dissolve deep-seated, long-held emotional patterns and beliefs.

Malachite's key vibrational property is its ability to bring to the surface deep-seated emotions so that they can be released. It is a carbonate that contains water and as such is useful in stimulating new developmental processes, thereby helping this client to 'let go and move on'. However, malachite brings suppressed feelings to the surface very quickly – it is a crystal that 'takes no prisoners'. To counter this effect, *rose quartz* was used at the same time as malachite at the same chakra and in the hands. The gentle energy of this pink crystal softens the less sympathetic effects of malachite and encourages forgiveness and unconditional love of the self and others. *Green malachite* and *pink rose quartz* both have a colour affinity with the heart chakra.

Deborah still comes regularly for re-balancing. Much has already been released and she is learning to acknowledge and let go of her old programming. She has recently reported that her bouts of IBS have been less frequent – and also that her feelings towards her mother are becoming more loving and less resentful.

George's case

George lives in a residential home and has suffered from chronic lower back pain for the past few years. He told me that he'd tried 'just about every pain killer under the sun' – with varying degrees of success but no real long-lasting pain relief. His condition had been investigated but no underlying medical cause had been found. He had heard from one of the other residents I had been seeing that crystals can relieve pain and he wanted to give it a try.

George was given a lower back massage using two large *amethyst* crystal palm stones. After ten minutes George said the pain was easing, and after a further ten minutes that it was completely gone.

Rationale for crystal choice

Amethyst is a member of the quartz family and is an oxide. Oxides produce energy which converts unstable states to stable ones. It is also a powerful pain-reliever and has the ability to release tension and encourage relaxation.

George returned for weekly sessions until he was hospitalised, sometime later, for a totally different and unconnected condition.

Jennifer's case

Jennifer is a successful businesswoman with a high-powered, stressful job. At our first meeting she revealed that her alcohol intake had increased sharply just recently, as a result of this, and also that she was not sleeping well. In addition, she was diagnosed with multiple sclerosis (relapsing/remitting) twelve years ago and although she is currently in remission she admitted that she was 'terrified of a relapse'. At the time of our meeting she had not been under direct medical supervision for several years. When I asked her why she had come to me and what she hoped to get from the session she was very clear. She replied 'the ability to relax and switch off so that my mind and body can recover and restore itself'. This response told me a lot. Here was a client who was ready and willing to take some responsibility for her own health and well-being; all she was asking for was the tools with which she might achieve this.

We discussed various techniques that I felt would be useful, including visualisation and home use of crystals. Jennifer was very open to both of these and said that she had some crystals at home but didn't know how to use them. It is not always the case that I can explain in detail to clients how crystals work in relation to their intrinsic vibrational energy and the human energy field, but I felt in this case that it would be beneficial., particularly if she was going to use crystals at home.

On checking her energy system I found that it was quite depleted on the physical level. Her base, sacral and solar plexus chakras were all out of balance at the physical level, while the third eye and crown chakras were out at the mental level. The heart chakra was also out of balance, but at the emotional level. We discussed the significance of all of these and I explained that the physical imbalance at the three lower chakras indicated low physical energy and vitality and also a lack of attention to caring for her bodily needs. At this point she admitted that she tended to eat on the run while at work, and sometimes she skipped meals altogether when time was short. This, I explained, seemed to be further confirmed by the heart chakra being out of balance at the emotional level indicating, in her case, a lack of self-care. The imbalance of the third eye and crown chakras at the mental level suggested, at this time, an inability to think as rationally and clearly as usual and also a likely diminishing sense of understanding and awareness. This caused her to frown and nod simultaneously, saying that she had only yesterday let her mind drift in an important meeting, which had resulted in her being caught on the hop when asked a question!

Red jasper was chosen for the base chakra, *carnelian* for the sacral chakra and *imperial topaz* for the solar plexus chakra. *Watermelon tourmaline* for the heart chakra, *amethyst* for the third eye chakra and double terminated *clear quartz* for the crown chakra.

To start, a visualisation was done to encourage relaxation and a quietening of the mind. Once the crystals were all placed on the body Jennifer started to really relax. After a few minutes she began to 'see' waves of colour lapping up her body; these were the colours red, orange, yellow, pink then green, blue, indigo then white. She understood without my telling her that these were the colours associated with each of the chakras and that what she was 'seeing' was the shifting of energy at each energy centre. At the appropriate time the crystals were removed and the session concluded.

Afterwards, I explained my rationale for crystal choice and advised Jennifer on the safe home use of one or two of her own crystals between sessions.

Rationale for crystal choice

Red jasper is quartz which contains other minerals, mainly iron oxide. It is sometimes referred to as 'the supreme nurturer' because it has the energetic properties of being able to stimulate circulation and enhance energy flow. It is an oxide and oxides have the ability to produce energy. The colour red has an affinity with the base chakra and is also stimulating.

Carnelian is also a quartz and an oxide and so has the same energetic properties as red jasper. In addition, it is of igneous formation and so is able to speed up processes. Its orange colour has an affinity with the sacral chakra.

Imperial topaz belongs to the orthorhombic system. Crystals of this system encourage inner peace and strength. It is an island silicate and has the properties of being able to aid in structuring one's life, even when under stress. In this case, it was chosen to help Jennifer maintain control over her life/work balance and also to support and fortify the nervous system, thus helping to maintain the status quo of her 'remission' phase. Its deep yellow colour has an affinity with the solar plexus chakra.

Watermelon tourmaline is green tourmaline with a red core. It is a ring silicate with a pillar structure and so has a stimulating property. It was chosen to stimulate regeneration of the nervous system and to encourage self-nurture. Its pink and green colours both have an affinity with the heart chakra.

Amethyst is a member of the quartz family and is an oxide. Oxides produce energy which converts unstable states to stable ones and as such is useful for addictive behaviour, such as excessive alcohol intake. It is also has the ability to release tension and encourage relaxation, and is a powerful aid for insomnia. Its purple colour has an affinity with the third eye chakra.

Clear quartz (double terminated). Clear quartz is a Master Healer and can be used on all energy centres and for all conditions. It was chosen to link all energy points in the central energy tube and to facilitate the flow of energy throughout the system in both directions. In addition, clear quartz brings clarity and focus – both are qualities which are needed at this time.

Jennifer continues to use crystals at home, under guidance, and to come for a therapy session when her busy schedule allows. She is still in remission.

Jean's case

Jean has worked as a nurse for several years, first in a hospital and then in a nursing home. Her back problems, she said, had started after the birth of her second child some years ago. Although the birth had been normal she had had a difficult labour as the baby lay against her spine, and she thought that this might have contributed to her current condition. She told me that she had been attending a chiropractor for treatment and, although the treatment was successful at re-aligning her spine and ultimately relieving pain, the effects did not last. This, she felt, was due to long hours spent on her feet as well as other physical requirements of her job. At the time of our meeting she had not had a treatment from the chiropractor for several weeks, but she told me that she was in considerable pain and discomfort

Jean was given a full spinal re-charge using two large *selenite* tumblestone crystals. The crystals were traced simultaneously along either side of the spinal column, the full length of the spine. Almost immediately she said that she felt a tingling sensation along the entire length of her spinal column – not unpleasant, just tingling and also a slight feeling of warmth. I explained that what she was experiencing was the energy flow in her central tube of energy being unblocked and restored. Afterwards, Jean said that the tingling had disappeared along with most of the pain and discomfort in her back. We discussed the benefits of further sessions and she still returns for therapy, as and when she feels the need.

Rationale for crystal choice

Selenite, a translucent form of gypsum, is a sulphate. As such, it has a calming effect on the nervous system and has the effect of being able to stabilise or dampen things.

It was chosen to stabilise the alignment of the spine and to dampen pain, while at the same time promoting flexibility and movement in the spinal column.

Important Note:

For confidentiality, ease of reading and for clarity of focus on the key aspects of each case described, I have not included full details of the crystals used or the information taken at each treatment.

For example, at every session a client case history, including lifestyle information, contra indications and any current medical information would be taken before a decision to offer therapy would be made.

In addition, all sessions would involve the use of grounding crystals and a crystal wand, as appropriate, and some may have involved the use of additional clear quartz crystals to amplify the effects of the crystals used.

Also, I have withheld any sensitive client interaction which might have occurred either before, during or after a session. These omissions have in no way distorted or affected the reporting of the cases as described.

References

Adey, WR & Bawin, SM: (1997) 'Brain interactions with weak electric and magnetic fields'. Oxford; Oxford University Press

Associated Press, Omaha World-Herald (1992) 'Tiny Crystal Magnets found in Human Brain'

Brennan, Barbara Ann (1987) ' Hands of Light', New York: Bantam Books

Choquette, Sonia (2000) 'Balancing your Chakras', London: Piatkus

Collins English Dictionary (2003), Complete and unabridged 6th Edition

Davies, Dr Brenda (1998), 'The Rainbow Journey', London: Hodder & Stoughton

Dorland, Frank (1992) 'Holy Ice': Bridge to the Subconscious', St. Paul, Minn: Galde Press Inc.

Foster, KR & Guy, AW (1986); 'The microwave problem'. Scientific American 255: pp531-532

Gienger, Michael (1998): 'Crystal Power, Crystal Healing: The Complete Handbook', London: Cassell & Co.

Gimbel, Theo (1997) 'Healing with Colour', London: Gaia Books

Greer, John Michael (2002) 'Techniques for geometric transformation,' USA: Llewellyn

Hall, Judy (2000) 'The Illustrated guide to Crystals', Hants: Godsfield Press

Hamilton, Dr David R. (2008) 'The Quantum Mind', www.drdavidhamilton.com (last accessed 13.02.10)

Hunt, Dr Valerie: www.valerievhunt.com (last accessed 28.01.10)

Judith, Anodea (1996) 'Eastern Body, Western Mind' Berkeley, CA: Celestial Arts

Kalmijn, AJ (1971) 'The electric sense of sharks and rays'. Journal of Experimental Biology 55: pp 371-383

Lawlor, Robert (1982) 'Sacred Geometry: Principles and Practice', London: Thames and Hudson

Morton, Chris & Thomas, Ceri Louise (1997) 'The Mystery of the Crystal Skulls', London: Thorsons

Pellant, Chris (1992) 'Rocks and Minerals', London: Dorling Kindersley

Reid, Lori (2000) 'Colour Book', London: Connections Book Publishing

Rennison, Susan Joy (2008) 'Tuning the Diamonds', Staffordshire: Joyfire Publishing

Simpson, Liz (1998) 'The book of Chakra Healing', London: Gaia Books

'The Living Matrix – The New Science of Healing' (2009): www.thelivingmatrixmovie.com

Warnke, U (1994) ' Electromagnetic sensitivity of animals and humans: Biological and clinical implications'. In: Ho MW, Popp, FA, Warnke, U 'Bioelectrodynamics and biocommunication.' Singapore: World Scientific

Washnis, G.J. & Hricak, R.Z. (1993)'Discovery of Magnetic Health, Rockville, MD: In Rennison, S.J. 'Tuning the Diamonds'. Staffordshire: Joyfire Publishing